ILLUSTRATED COURSE GUIDES

W9-BUI-826

Teamwork and
Team Building

SECOND EDITION

ILLUSTRATED COURSE GUIDES

Teamwork and Team Building

SECOND EDITION

Jeff Butterfield

CENGAGE

Australia • Brazil • Canada • Mexico • Singapore • United Kingdom • United States

CENGAGE

Teamwork and Team Building, **2nd Edition:**
Illustrated Course Guides
Jeff Butterfield

Product Director: Kathleen McMahon

Associate Product Manager: Reed Curry

Associate Content Developer: Maria Garguilo

Marketing Director: Michele McTighe

Marketing Manager: Jeff Tousignant

Marketing Coordinator: Cassie Cloutier

Contributing Author: Lisa Ruffolo

Developmental Editor: Lisa Ruffolo

Content Project Manager: Jen Feltri-George

IP Analyst: Amber Hill

Senior IP Project Manager: Kathy Kucharek

Proofreader: Brandy Lilly

Indexer: Elizabeth Cunningham

Print Buyer: Fola Orekoya

Composition: Lumina Datamatics Inc.

Art Director: Diana Graham

Cover Template Designer: Lisa Kuhn, Curio Press, LLC www.curiopress.com

Text Designer: GEX Publishing Services

For product information and technology assistance, contact us at
Cengage Customer & Sales Support, 1-800-354-9706
or support.cengage.com.

For permission to use material from this text or product, submit all requests online at **www.cengage.com/permissions.**

Library of Congress Control Number: 2016938487

ISBN-13: 978-1-337-11927-6
ISBN-10: 1-337-11927-x

Cengage
200 Pier 4 Boulevard
Boston, MA 02210
USA

Cengage is a leading provider of customized learning solutions with employees residing in nearly 40 different countries and sales in more than 125 countries around the world. Find your local representative at: **www.cengage.com.**

To learn more about Cengage platforms and services, register or access your online learning solution, or purchase materials for your course, visit **www.cengage.com.**

The following photos are used under license from Shutterstock.com:
Figure A-3a © Sean Prior, 2010.
Figure A-3b © Yuri Arcurs, 2010.
Figure A-3c © Yuri Arcurs, 2010.
Figure A-4a © Stephen Coburn, 2010.
Figure A-9 © Andresr, 2010.
Figure E-1 © Andresr, 2010.
All other photos © Jupiterimages Corporation.

Printed in the United States of America
Print Number: 09   Print Year: 2021

About the Series

Students work hard to earn certificates and degrees to prepare for a particular career—but do they have the soft skills necessary to succeed in today's digital workplace? Can they communicate effectively? Present themselves professionally? Work in a team? Industry leaders agree there is a growing need for these essential soft skills; in fact, they are critical to a student's success in the workplace. Without them, they will struggle and even fail. However, students entering the workforce who can demonstrate strong soft skills have a huge competitive advantage.

The *Illustrated Course Guides—Soft Skills for a Digital Workplace* series is designed to help you teach these important skills, better preparing your students to enter a competitive marketplace. Here are some of the key elements you will find in each book in the series:

• Focused content allows for flexibility: Each book in the series is short, focused, and covers only the most essential skills related to the topic. You can use the modular content in standalone courses or workshops or you can integrate it into existing courses.

• Visual design keeps students engaged: Our unique pedagogical design presents each skill on two facing pages, with key concepts and instructions on the left and illustrations on the right. This keeps students of all levels on track.

• Varied activities put skills to the test: Each book includes hands-on activities, team exercises, critical thinking questions, and scenario-based activities to allow students to put their skills to work and demonstrate their retention of the material.

Read the Preface for more details on the key pedagogical elements and features of this book. We hope the books in this series help your students gain the critical soft skills they need to succeed in whatever career they choose.

Advisory Board

We thank our Advisory Board who gave us their opinions and guided our decisions as we developed the first titles in this series. They are as follows:

Debi Griggs, Instructor of Business and Business Technology, Bellevue College

Jean Insinga, Professor of Information Systems, Middlesex Community College

Gary Marrer, CIS Faculty, Glendale Community College

Linda Meccouri, Professor, Springfield Technical Community College

Lynn Wermers, Chair, Computer and Information Sciences, North Shore Community College

Nancy Wilson Head, Executive Director Teaching & Learning Technologies, Purdue University

Preface

Welcome to *Teamwork and Team Building, Second Edition: Illustrated Course Guides*. If this is your first experience with the Illustrated Course Guides, you'll see that this book has a unique design: each skill is presented on two facing pages, with Essential Elements on the left and illustrations and examples pictured on the right. The layout makes it easy to learn a skill without having to read a lot of text and flip pages to see an illustration. The design also makes this a great reference after the course is over! See the illustration on the right to learn more about the pedagogical and design elements of a typical lesson.

Focused on the Essentials

Each two-page lesson presents only the most important information about the featured lesson skill. The left page of the lesson presents 5 or 6 key Essential Elements, which are the most important guidelines that a student needs to know about the skill. Absorbing and retaining a limited number of key ideas makes it more likely that students will retain and apply the skill in a real-life situation.

Hands-On Activities

Every lesson contains a You Try It exercise, where students demonstrate their understanding of the lesson skill by completing a task that relates to it. The steps in the You Try It exercises are often general, requiring that students use critical thinking to complete the task.

Real World Advice and Examples

To help put lesson skills in context, many lessons contain yellow shaded boxes that present real-world stories pulled from today's workplace. Some lessons also contain Do's and Don'ts tables, featuring key guidelines on what to do and not do in certain workplace situations relating to the lesson skill. The Technology@Work lesson at the end of every unit covers Web 2.0 tools and other technologies relating to the unit.

Each two-page spread focuses on a single skill.

Short introduction reviews key lesson points and presents a real-world case study to engage students.

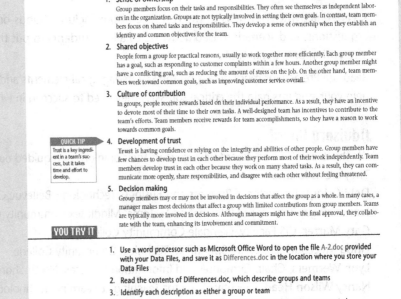

Lessons and Exercises

Every lesson features large illustrations of examples discussed in the lessons.

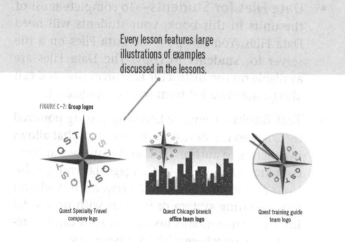

FIGURE C-7: Group logos

| Quest Specialty Travel company logo | Quest Chicago branch office team logo | Quest training guide team logo |

TABLE C-4: Creating a team identity do's and don'ts

guideline	do	don't
Name your team	Select an appropriate and easy-to-remember name in a team meeting	**Don't** choose a name that might offend anyone in or outside of the company
Use images to build an identity	• Create a team logo • Use the logo on anything the team produces • Print the team slogan on a poster or banner • Post signs with the team name and logo where the team works • Add the team name and logo to items that can be used as incentive gifts	• **Don't** select a logo without involving all of the team members • **Don't** force your team identity where others might resent it

Using social networks for team building

Companies large and small are using social networks to market their products and connect with customers. Some are also using the same Web tools to create internal networks for teams. Younger workers in particular are comfortable with the tools provided by a social network. Teams in general can quickly establish an identity and simplify communication. Companies are finding that social networks are an efficient way for teams to get to know one another, share information, and recruit others to the team. However, as Heather Green writes in a recent *BusinessWeek* article, "Setting up a corporate version of a social network has its own challenges, as well. Companies have to build in safeguards to ensure that they can track the discussions and document sharing, to be certain that employees comply with government regulations and don't tumble into legal hot water." One of the main benefits of using an internal social network is decreasing e-mail traffic. Social networks make collaboration easy. Green relates the case of the Film Foundation in Los Angeles, which is using a team to manage an educational film program. "Workers can archive research documents, share calendars, chat, and blog. A team of 60 researchers, writers, teachers, and filmmakers is putting together a curriculum, distributed free to schools across the country that teaches students how to understand the visual language of films. By having members brainstorm, review each other's work, and prepare budgets on the network, the Film Foundation believes it can cut by half the amount of time it takes to create the materials."

Source: Green, Heather, "In-House Social Networks," *BusinessWeek,* September 23, 2007.

Building and Developing Teams   **Teamwork 59**

Teamwork

News to Use boxes provide real-world stories related to the lesson topic.

Do's & Don'ts table present key tips for what to do and not to do.

The lessons use Quest Specialty Travel, a fictional adventure travel company, as the case study. The assignments on the light purple pages at the end of each unit increase in difficulty. Data files and case studies provide a variety of interesting and relevant business applications. Assignments include:

- **Soft Skills Reviews** provide multiple choice questions that test students' understanding of the unit material.

- **Critical Thinking Questions** pose topics for discussion that require analysis and evaluation. Many also challenge students to consider and react to realistic critical thinking and application of the unit skills.

- **Independent Challenges** are case projects requiring critical thinking and application of the unit skills.

- **Real Life Independent Challenges** are practical exercises where students can apply the skills they learned in an activity that will help their own lives. For instance, they might analyze decisions they need to make, such as which job offer to accept, whether to buy a house or rent an apartment, and whether to continue their formal education.

- **Team Challenges** are practical projects that require working together in a team to solve a problem.

- **Be the Critic Exercises** are activities that require students to evaluate a flawed example and provide ideas for improving it.

Instructor Resources

The Instructor Resources provide instructors with a wide range of tools that enhance teaching and learning. These resources and more can be accessed from the instructor companion site. Log in at www.cengage.com/SSO.

- **Instructor's Manual**—Written by the author and available as an electronic file, the Instructor's Manual is a valuable teaching tool for your course. It includes detailed lecture topics with teaching tips for each unit.

- **Sample Syllabus**—Prepare and customize your course easily using this sample course outline.

- **PowerPoint Presentations**—Each unit has a corresponding PowerPoint presentation that you can use in lecture, distribute to your students, or customize to suit your course.

- **Solutions to Exercises**—Solutions to Exercises contains every file students are asked to create or modify in the lessons and end-of-unit material. This section also includes a solutions to the Soft Skills Reviews and Independent Challenges.

- **Data Files for Students**—To complete most of the units in this book, your students will need Data Files. You can post the Data Files on a file server for students to copy. The Data Files are available on the Instructor Resources site, and can also be downloaded from www.cengage.com.

- **Test Banks**—Cengage Learning Testing powered by Cognero is a flexible, online system that allows instructors to author, edit, and manage test bank content from multiple Cengage Learning solutions and to create multiple versions. It works on any operating system or browser with no special installs or downloads needed, so tests can be created from anywhere with Internet access.

Brief Contents

Contents

Unit E: Managing Meetings   97

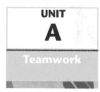

Working in Groups and Teams

Files You Will Need:

A-1.doc
A-2.doc
A-3.doc
A-4.doc
A-5.doc
A-6.doc
A-7.doc
A-8.doc
A-9.doc
A-10.pptx

Companies in the United States and in other countries are now using groups and teams to become more competitive. In business, groups and teams often develop new products and services. They also correct problems and improve quality, make recommendations and decisions, and work on complex projects. Successful teams can complete more tasks and produce more high-quality results than a person working alone. A high-performing team can achieve even more than the combined talents of the group members. However, not all teams are effective. A 1994 study by A.T. Kearny found that as many as 9 out of 10 teams are ineffective, meaning they fail to complete their assigned tasks. In this unit, you learn about the role of teams in organizations and what makes teams successful. Quest Specialty Travel is opening a new branch office in Chicago, Illinois. Don Novak is the head of the branch and is assembling a small staff to open the office by March of next year. Don hires you as the assistant office manager, and wants you to help him form the new staff into an effective team.

OBJECTIVES

Understand the role of teams in organizations

Define types of groups and teams

Recognize differences between groups and teams

Ensure team success

Empower teams

Earn rewards for team effort

Become a high-performing team

Work with distributed teams

Understanding the Role of Teams in Organizations

The success of the Japanese auto industry a few decades ago made teams popular in business. Before that, employers viewed each worker as an independent labor resource. However, when people work together in a group, they can have a greater sense of purpose and complete more tasks than they do on their own. Teams often include people with varied backgrounds and skills. They give the group a rich set of talents and abilities to focus on their assigned tasks. ⬛⬛⬛⬛ Before working with Don Novak to help him encourage teamwork at Quest, you decide to learn about the role of teams in organizations.

DETAILS

Organizations use teams because:

- **Teams can reflect the larger organization**

  In most medium-size and large companies, employees work in a department or division, such as customer service or marketing. A team can include members from many departments, such as one from customer service, another from marketing, and another from accounting. Each team member approaches company goals from the point of view of their department, while learning other points of view. These diverse teams reflect the diversity of the larger organization, which can help solve problems and meet goals.

- **Teams can complete projects that are too big for one person**

  One person can complete only a certain number of tasks during a work day. A single person also has a fixed set of talents, limited resources, and incomplete information about the company's history. On the other hand, a team can handle the demands of larger and more complicated projects. Although one person manages the group, members can perform tasks best suited to their talents, skills, and knowledge. A team can handle work that would be impractical for a single person.

  For example, suppose a team at Quest Specialty Travel is planning the grand opening of the new branch office in Chicago. The team needs to complete many tasks, such as sending invitations to customers, creating and placing ads, requesting prizes for a raffle, and ordering banners. As Figure A-1 shows, four team members can work on these tasks at the same time, accomplishing much more in one day than a single person can.

- **Teams can create a broad range of solutions**

  QUICK TIP
  Teams are not cooperative automatically; they need to develop a collective identity before they can solve problems creatively.

  When a group of people works together cooperatively, they can draw on a large pool of ideas and abilities to solve problems. For example, suppose a team includes members from three departments. The team is supposed to recommend new tours for Quest Specialty Travel. See Figure A-2. Gina considers what customers will like most. Kevin thinks about the practical details of scheduling. Lee considers all the tours Quest offers, and whether the new ones they recommend will be different. Together, Gina and Kevin will think of tours that are convenient for customers. Gina and Lee will suggest unique tours that meet customer requests. Kevin and Lee might offer ideas for tours scheduled to showcase special events in new destinations. All three members will recommend tours that are convenient, popular, and well designed.

- **Teams create a sense of obligation, commitment, and motivation**

  The military uses the term **esprit de corps** (pronounced *espree d core*) to describe the increased motivation and morale that develops when people depend on each other. Business teams can also develop esprit de corps when members are part of an effort that the company values and respects.

- **Teams make decisions that others are willing to accept**

  Teams often identify solutions and make decisions that affect the company in some way. When the team includes members from each part of the company, especially those affected by the decisions, the whole company tends to be more accepting of the outcomes. A team or committee can be more democratic than a single executive making a decision.

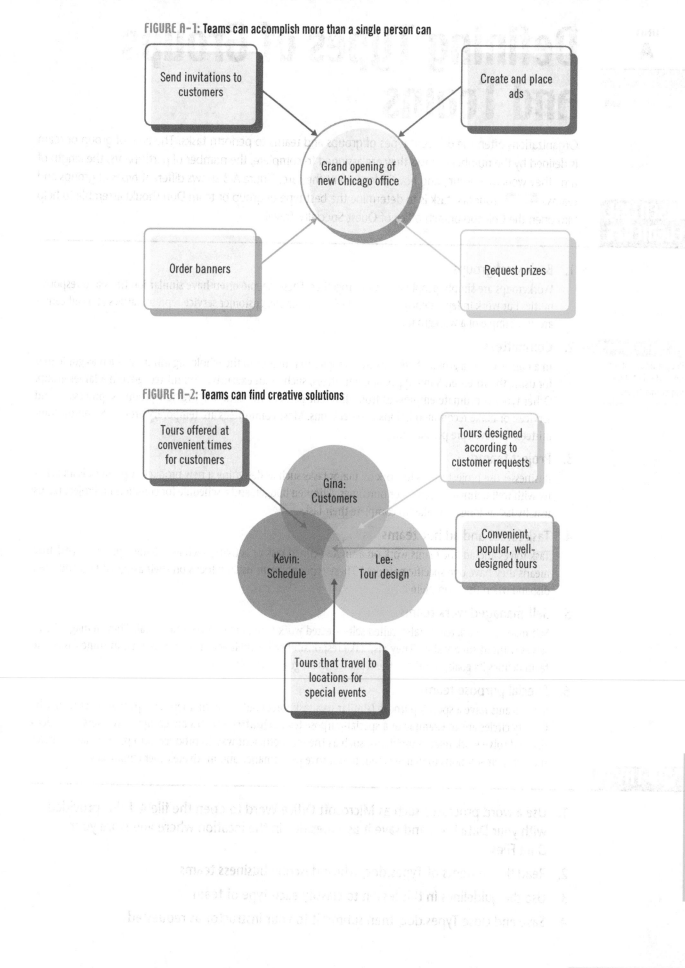

FIGURE A-1: Teams can accomplish more than a single person can

Send invitations to customers

Create and place ads

Grand opening of new Chicago office

Order banners

Request prizes

FIGURE A-2: Teams can find creative solutions

Tours offered at convenient times for customers

Tours designed according to customer requests

Gina: Customers

Convenient, popular, well-designed tours

Kevin: Schedule

Lee: Tour design

Tours that travel to locations for special events

Defining Types of Groups and Teams

Organizations often use different types of groups and teams to perform tasks. The type of group or team is defined by the number of tasks they are assigned to complete, the number of participants, the length of time they work as a group, and how independent they are. Figure A-3 shows different types of groups and teams. Your first task is to determine the best type of group or team Don should assemble to help him open the Chicago branch office of Quest Specialty Travel.

ESSENTIAL ELEMENTS

1. **Basic workgroups**

   Workgroups are simply people who work together. These people often have similar job titles and responsibilities but work independently of each other. For example, customer service representatives at a call center are an example of a workgroup.

   QUICK TIP
   People often rotate on and off of standing committees.

2. **Committees**

   In a **committee**, a group of people discuss topics that matter to the whole organization, such as guidelines for using the Internet. Some types of committees, such as an executive committee, govern a larger group. Other types coordinate employees from different parts of the company; review products, processes, and services; or make recommendations and decisions. Most committees are temporary groups. Standing committees, however, are permanent.

3. **Project teams**

   Businesses use project teams to work on major tasks such as designing a new product. A **project** is an activity with well-defined objectives or outcomes, a limited budget, and a schedule for completion. Project teams usually last as long as it takes to complete their tasks.

4. **Task forces and ad hoc teams**

   Task forces and ad hoc teams work on a single defined task or activity, such as solving a problem. (**Ad hoc** means they have one specific purpose.) These types of teams usually focus on their assigned task and then disband when they complete it.

5. **Self-managed work teams**

   Self-managed work teams (also called self-directed work teams) have a common goal. They manage themselves without supervision. They also take responsibility for their activities and results. In some cases, the team defines its goals; in others, the team works on goals that others set.

6. **Special-purpose teams**

   Some teams have a special purpose (similar to a task force) but are permanent groups that meet regularly. Quality circles are an example of a special-purpose team. **Quality circles** are groups of workers who identify and solve work-related problems, such as the most efficient way to produce auto parts. Quality circles present their solutions to management to improve performance and motivate other employees.

YOU TRY IT

1. Use a word processor such as Microsoft Office Word to open the file A-1.doc provided with your Data Files, and save it as Types.doc in the location where you store your Data Files

2. Read the contents of Types.doc, which describe business teams

3. Use the guidelines in this lesson to classify each type of team

4. Save and close Types.doc, then submit it to your instructor as requested

FIGURE A-3: Types of groups and teams

A work group contains people with similar job titles and responsibilities

A committee is a group of people who discuss topics that matter to the whole organization

Businesses use project teams to work on major tasks

Quality circles are groups of workers who identify and solve work-related problems

Quality circles

Quality circles are small groups ranging from 3–12 people who do similar work. Someone experienced with quality circles trains them before they start meeting. Then members meet voluntarily for about 1 hour per week, and are usually paid for their time. The main tasks are to identify problems at work and suggest solutions. Japanese firms introduced the idea of quality circles, and they became popular in American businesses in the 1980s. Many major corporations set them up, and then they fell out of favor. According to the *Economist*, "A study in 1988 found that 80 percent of a sample of large companies in the West that had introduced quality circles in the early 1980s had abandoned them before the end of the decade." Why did such a popular technique quickly lose popularity? Companies embraced the idea as a fad, but didn't make the types of changes that would support true quality circles, which use collective wisdom to solve problems. For example, some companies trained only managers to run quality circles, not the staff who participated in them. Others set up quality circles that maintained lines of authority. For example, managers were leaders while administrative staff took minutes. Quality circles were designed to set aside lines of authority. The most major error was ignoring real problems in the business (such as not meeting customer needs) and focusing on trivia.

Source: Staff, "Quality Circle," *Economist.com*, November 4, 2009.

Teamwork

Recognizing Differences Between Groups and Teams

People often use the terms *group* and *team* interchangeably, but the two terms have practical differences. **Teams** have a shared sense of purpose. They build strength and competence from the relationships between members. A **group** is a number of people who work on similar tasks or follow the same procedures. See Figure A-4. In other words, a team is a group that has become unified over time, usually through team-building efforts. Table A-1 summarizes the similarities and differences between groups and teams. During your first meeting with Don and the new Chicago staff, you discuss the differences between groups and teams.

1. ### Sense of ownership

   Group members focus on their tasks and responsibilities. They often see themselves as independent laborers in the organization. Groups are not typically involved in setting their own goals. In contrast, team members focus on shared tasks and responsibilities. They develop a sense of ownership when they establish an identity and common objectives for the team.

2. ### Shared objectives

   People form a group for practical reasons, usually to work together more efficiently. Each group member has a goal, such as responding to customer complaints within a few hours. Another group member might have a conflicting goal, such as reducing the amount of stress on the job. On the other hand, team members work toward common goals, such as improving customer service overall.

3. ### Culture of contribution

   In groups, people receive rewards based on their individual performance. As a result, they have an incentive to devote most of their time to their own tasks. A well-designed team has incentives to contribute to the team's efforts. Team members receive rewards for team accomplishments, so they have a reason to work towards common goals.

QUICK TIP

Trust is a key ingredient in a team's success, but it takes time and effort to develop.

4. ### Development of trust

   Trust is having confidence or relying on the integrity and abilities of other people. Group members have few chances to develop trust in each other because they perform most of their work independently. Team members develop trust in each other because they work on many shared tasks. As a result, they can communicate more openly, share responsibilities, and disagree with each other without feeling threatened.

5. ### Decision making

   Group members may or may not be involved in decisions that affect the group as a whole. In many cases, a manager makes most decisions that affect a group with limited contributions from group members. Teams are typically more involved in decisions. Although managers might have the final approval, they collaborate with the team, enhancing its involvement and commitment.

YOU TRY IT

1. Use a word processor such as Microsoft Office Word to open the file A-2.doc provided with your Data Files, and save it as Differences.doc in the location where you store your Data Files

2. Read the contents of Differences.doc, which describe groups and teams

3. Identify each description as either a group or team

4. Save and close Differences.doc, then submit it to your instructor as requested

A group of computer technicians individually repair and maintain customer computers

A team of construction workers cooperate to erect a building

TABLE A-1: Differences between groups and teams

characteristic	group	team
Definition	Collection of individuals	Unified group working together to meet common goals
Focus	Individual tasks and responsibilities	Shared tasks and responsibilities
Objectives	Differ from one member to another	Same for all members
Rewards	Based on individual accomplishments	Based on team accomplishments
Trust	Few chances to develop trust	Shared tasks offer many chances to develop trust
Decisions	Often not involved in decisions that affect the group	Make decisions or collaborate with a decision maker

Collegial conflict resolution

A **colleague** is someone who holds the same type of job as you do and usually works in the same company. In this sense, a colleague is a coworker. Your colleague can also be united with you in common purpose, respecting your professional abilities. When you are being collegial with someone else, you are acting like this second meaning of colleague—you work cooperatively with someone else with trust and respect. This doesn't mean that colleagues don't disagree or have conflicts. Conflict is a common part of organizational life.

Both groups and teams experience conflict. The way they resolve conflicts, however, tends to differ. Because group members rely on managers to set the direction of their work day, they also rely on management to resolve conflicts. Team members are more inclined to resolve their own conflicts. A well-functioning team might even see conflict as an opportunity to openly communicate, resolve differences, and explore new ideas. Team members often give up individual benefits or resources for the sake of the common good.

Ensuring Team Success

When a team is properly formed, developed, and managed, it can produce incredible results. For example, teams can achieve larger, more complex goals than a single person or group can. Teams can also increase cooperation among competing groups. However, successful teamwork is not automatic, nor is it as easy as it might seem. Building effective teams takes ongoing effort and commitment. Table A-2 lists the do's and don'ts for ensuring team success. Don Novak has asked you and the five members of the Chicago staff to work together as a team to open the new branch of Quest Specialty Travel. He meets with the team to plan how to ensure success.

1. Discuss the team goals

One of the key characteristics that defines a team and differentiates it from a group is that the members share the same goals. The team itself should play a significant role in determining these goals. Management can define the outcomes, but the team should decide how to accomplish them.

QUICK TIP

When everyone understands their roles and those of the other members, a group begins to work as a team.

2. Clearly understand each member's roles and expectations

In a well-functioning team, members serve different roles. Common roles include leader, creative thinker, facilitator, peacemaker, detail recorder, and specialist. See Figure A-5. As a group develops into a team, people adopt the roles and responsibilities that suit their abilities. In some cases, a team leader might ask someone to assume a necessary role that has been overlooked.

3. Let a team member emerge as the leader

A good team leader can create a healthy and positive work environment, motivate and inspire the team members, and support the team in general so it reaches its goals. Often, the best team leaders emerge from the ranks of the team itself. Leaders not only keep the focus on tasks the team needs to perform, they also pay attention to how the team itself is working. For example, if the Chicago team for Quest works many extra hours to open the new branch office, they might meet their goals on schedule. However, if no one pays attention to how team members feel about working the extra hours, they are likely to experience high turnover.

QUICK TIP

Set ground rules that allow for open and frank discussions.

4. Show respect for differences

Teams can bring together people with different perspectives, abilities, and ideas. This gives the team a much broader base of knowledge, creativity, and skills than any single person could have. However, a team should guard against intolerance for ideas and opinions that are at odds with the popular position. Teams should actively strive to welcome and respect different ways of thinking about and completing tasks.

5. Create a sense of urgency

Several studies find that teams perform better when members have a sense of urgency about their work. For example, some teams rise to the occasion to meet a tight deadline. Others respond positively when the team members are competing with an outside group.

1. Use a word processor such as Microsoft Office Word to open the file A-3.doc provided with your Data Files, and save it as Success.doc in the location where you store your Data Files

2. Read the contents of Success.doc, which describe a business team

3. Recommend what the team should do to ensure success

4. Save and close Success.doc, then submit it to your instructor as requested

FIGURE A-5: Typical team roles

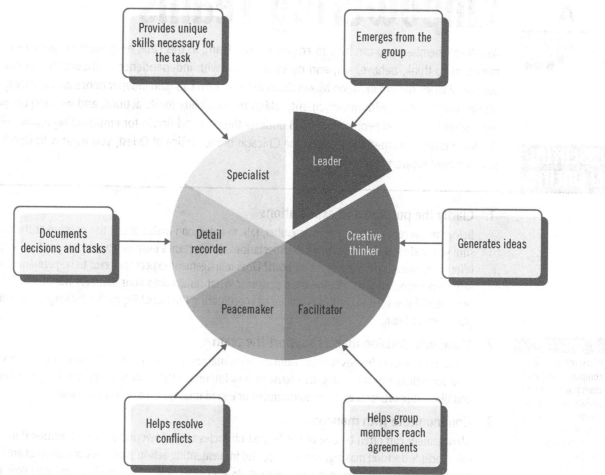

Provides unique skills necessary for the task

Emerges from the group

Specialist — Leader

Documents decisions and tasks — Detail recorder

Creative thinker — Generates ideas

Peacemaker — Facilitator

Helps resolve conflicts

Helps group members reach agreements

TABLE A-2: Ensuring team success do's and don'ts

guideline	do	don't
Discuss goals	• Decide how to accomplish the team's goals • Accept responsibility for meeting the goals	**Don't** wait for managers to set the goals
Understand roles and expectations	• Let team members adopt roles that suit their abilities • Respect these roles within the team	• **Don't** overlook an important role that no team member has assumed • **Don't** take over someone's role, but don't be afraid to help with some roles, such as thinking creatively and reaching agreements
Find a leader	• Look for a team member who can focus on the team's tasks and dynamics at the same time • Use a coordinator until a leader emerges	• **Don't** automatically make the highest-ranking person the leader • **Don't** avoid necessary tasks until a leader emerges—discuss who should complete them
Respect differences	• Take advantage of the different perspectives, abilities, and ideas offered in a team • Encourage differences to avoid intolerance or overlooking new ideas	• **Don't** fall into the trap of encouraging only familiar ideas • **Don't** discourage new ways of thinking
Create urgency	• Look for ways to create urgency, such as rallying to meet a deadline • Compete with other groups or standards	• **Don't** keep up the urgency for long periods • **Don't** invent a reason to be urgent about team tasks

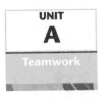

Empowering Teams

As a team member, you can help to empower your team. In this case, **empower** means to enable team members to think, behave, act, and make decisions with independence. Although teams can only be successful when the organization allows them to be, a team can gain independence and authority by communicating regularly with management, taking responsibility for its actions, and working cooperatively with other groups and people. Table A-3 outlines the do's and don'ts for empowering teams. As the team is being formed for opening the Chicago branch office of Quest, you meet with Don to discuss management support for the team.

1. Clarify the purpose and expectations

Before you accept a role as a team member, talk to a decision maker about the purpose of the team. Make sure you understand your employer's expectations. Is the team's purpose to identify production problems, offer suggestions for solving them, or both? Does management expect the team to be permanent or temporary? What types of tasks will the team perform? What results does your manager want to see? How much time should you spend meeting as a team or coordinating the team? Figure A-6 lists typical reasons a company forms a team.

2. Make sure decision makers support the team

> **QUICK TIP**
> When others in the company know your team is working on a project important to senior management, they are usually more cooperative and helpful.

Without clear and obvious support from decision makers, a team is unlikely to accomplish much. Talk to your immediate supervisor to gain a sense of how important the team is to upper managers. Look for clear and direct support, such as an announcement or e-mail message from a decision maker.

3. Communicate with managers

Management can often be one of the biggest obstacles to empowering a team. Traditional management roles include decision making, authorizing, and implementing action plans. Many managers are hesitant to hand these responsibilities over to employees. As a member of a team, keep in touch with your managers. Tell them about the team's progress. Explain how you are overcoming problems. Describe the solutions you found. Keep your manager involved in your activities without burdening him or her with too many details.

4. Identify roadblocks and barriers

> **QUICK TIP**
> Instead of telling your boss you have a problem, say that you have some ideas for solving one.

Every team faces obstacles as they work on their tasks and assignments. For example, your team might have trouble getting the equipment or information it needs. A new idea your team tries actually slows the pace of work instead of improving it. Instead of letting these roadblocks interrupt the team's progress, identify the problem with your team. Discuss possible solutions. Before taking action to overcome a major barrier, present the problem and solutions to your manager so you can work cooperatively to solve the problem.

5. Ask for authorization

Empowered teams make decisions, access resources, and take actions to accomplish their goals. A manager in your company can authorize your team in advance to make the decisions they need. If your manager seems reluctant to grant this type of advance approval, start with minor matters, such as setting a schedule for team meetings on your own.

1. Use a word processor such as Microsoft Office Word to open the file **A-4.doc** provided with your Data Files, and save it as Authorize.doc in the location where you store your Data Files

2. Read the contents of Authorize.doc, which describe a business team

3. Describe what the team can do to be more successful in its company

4. Save and close Authorize.doc, then submit it to your instructor as requested

FIGURE A-6: Reasons organizations form teams

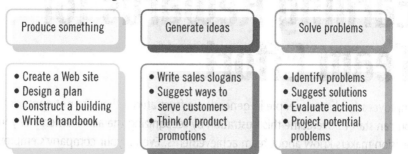

Produce something	Generate ideas	Solve problems
• Create a Web site • Design a plan • Construct a building • Write a handbook	• Write sales slogans • Suggest ways to serve customers • Think of product promotions	• Identify problems • Suggest solutions • Evaluate actions • Project potential problems

TABLE A-3: Empowering teams do's and don'ts

guideline	do	don't
Clarify the purpose	• Talk to a decision maker about the purpose of the team • Make sure you understand the organization's expectations	**Don't** assume you know why the team is being formed
Look for management support	• Make sure decision makers support the team • Talk to your immediate supervisor about the team • Watch for announcements or messages from upper management	**Don't** commit to a team that has little support from management
Communicate with managers	• Be aware that empowered teams can threaten traditional management roles • Keep in touch with your managers • Provide updates on the team's progress • Describe solutions	**Don't** burden your manager with too many details about the team's activities or internal discussions
Identify obstacles	• Discuss problems with the team as soon as possible • Suggest likely solutions • Complete some preliminary work before presenting a problem and solutions to your manager	**Don't** present a problem to a manager without possible solutions
Ask for authorization	• Ask for approval before you need it • If necessary, request authority to make minor decisions before major ones	**Don't** interrupt your team's progress by waiting for approval

Empowered teams make a difference

In the mid-1990s, British Airways had a customer service problem. If customer complaints were handled within a few days of the complaint, most customers were satisfied, and usually bought another ticket from British Airways. However, the average amount of time for British Airways to respond was 12 weeks. By then, customers were more difficult to satisfy and often demanded full compensation for problems such as cancelled flights and lost luggage. To solve their customer service problem, British Airways installed a new computer system and empowered the team that handled complaints. The new policy encouraged customer service team members to use their judgment when resolving complaints. The team could "take ownership of the problems" and offer solutions directly on the phone. The team used the new computer system to learn about their customers, which made them more sympathetic and apologetic when handling complaints. Because British Airways empowered the customer service team, customer satisfaction increased. Customers also requested lower compensation for problems. Job satisfaction for the customer relations team members also increased from around 20 percent to 69 percent. The empowered customer relations team made a big difference for British Airways.

Source: Staff, "The Support Structure of Empowered Teams," Team Building Web site, *www.teambuildingportal.com*, accessed January 11, 2010.

Teamwork

Earning Rewards for Team Effort

Employees (and most people in general) are frustrated if they are not appreciated for the work they do. You can start to overcome this frustration by recognizing the achievements of your teammates. Make sure decision makers know about team achievements. Even if your company's employee recognition program is designed to reward individual efforts, not team efforts, you can work to change that culture gradually. Raising the visibility of your team will help earn rewards over time. Table A-4 summarizes the do's and don'ts of earning rewards for team effort. ⬛⬛⬛⬛ You and Don discuss how your team can earn rewards for their work on opening a new branch office.

1. Promote your team

Changing a company's culture takes time, patience, and sustained effort. As a team member, you can promote your team's efforts. Do so by praising the accomplishments of your team and other teams in the company. Look for ways to make your team more visible to decision makers. For example, accept difficult tasks or offer to train new employees in an area related to your team's goals.

2. Review evaluations

Before starting to work with a team, review the company's procedures for employee review. If the evaluations clearly recognize and reward team effort, share this information with team members. On the other hand, if the review process doesn't cover team efforts, be sure to mention your team activities and accomplishments during your review. Many companies ask employees to complete a self-evaluation (also called a self-appraisal) before a review. Figure A-7 shows a typical self-evaluation form. This offers a chance to clearly show what you and your team have accomplished.

3. Encourage your team to exceed expectations

If your company rewards teams and individuals for meeting and exceeding goals, encourage your team to perform better than expected. Discuss your team's performance during team meetings, and restate your goals. Also seek feedback from managers about your team's performance. This request indicates that you care about your performance and want to be successful.

4. Determine what types of recognition are rewarding to you

Some employees are primarily motivated by financial rewards. Other employees place a higher value on nonfinancial rewards such as public recognition or flexible scheduling. Understand what works for you. During reviews and other opportunities, mention what motivates you and your team. Your manager might need to know what incentives are appropriate.

5. Be generous with appreciation

One of the most powerful rewards you can give to your coworkers is an expression of appreciation for their work. Thanking team members for their efforts helps to build team unity. It also encourages others to extend the same recognition to you.

1. Use a word processor such as Microsoft Office Word to open the file **A-5.doc** provided with your Data Files, and save it as Reward.doc in the location where you store your Data Files

2. Read the contents of Reward.doc, which describe a team project

3. Identify appropriate rewards for the members of the team

4. Save and close Reward.doc, then submit it to your instructor as requested

Quest Specialty Travel

Employee Self-Evaluation

Employee Information			
Employee Name:	Amy Jamison	Employee ID:	65036
Job Title:	Assistant Office Manager	Date:	May 23, 2013
Manager:	Don Novak	Branch:	Chicago
Review Period:	1/1/2013 to 6/1/2013		

Goals

- Describe the goals you set out to accomplish for this review period:

Create master schedule for office opening
Manage time efficiently
Set up ongoing team meetings

- Which goals did you accomplish?

Created and revised master schedule
Now meeting weekly with team

Quest Specialty Travel

TABLE A-4: Earning rewards for team effort do's and don'ts

guideline	do	don't
Promote teams	• Praise your teammates and their accomplishments • Make your team more visible to decision makers	**Don't** try to change company culture too abruptly
Review evaluations	• Read the company's policy for employee review • Share information with your teammates • During a review, ask your manager what your team can do to earn rewards	**Don't** dismiss your team's achievements if your company doesn't immediately reward them
Exceed expectations	• Encourage your team to perform better than expected • Discuss team performance during team meetings • Restate team goals so they are fresh to all team members • Seek feedback from managers	**Don't** try to guess how well your team is doing; show that you care about being successful
Reward your team	• Think about what motivates you • Identify what motivates your team • Mention these motivations to your manager • Thank your teammates for the work they do	**Don't** hold back on your appreciation—others will also reflect that appreciation back to you

Teamwork

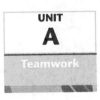
Becoming a High-Performing Team

Every so often, a team comes together and delivers in unexpected ways. So-called **high-performing teams** are made up of people who develop chemistry with each other and work together very effectively. This type of group meets all the qualifications of a regular team, but the members have a higher commitment to the team than usual. Although any area can have high-performing teams, most are involved with improving or designing products, services, and company processes. Now that you are working with the staff at the Chicago branch of Quest Specialty Travel as a team, you want to know what it takes to become a high-performing team.

ESSENTIAL ELEMENTS

1. Use the best ingredients

The quality of a team comes from the quality of its parts. If you are helping to assemble a team, suggest people that have been successful in other groups. As a team member, focus on the skills you have that complement the skills of other people in your team.

2. Participate actively

QUICK TIP

High-performing teams are more likely to dismiss passive members and recruit others that can contribute actively.

High-performing teams expect everyone's active involvement. If you are an active team member, ask less active people to help you complete tasks. If you are not as active as others, volunteer to accept responsibilities or offer to help others.

3. Emphasize cohesiveness

A **cohesive** team works closely together. Team members feel connected to other members. They spend time working together and do best when their work spaces are near each other. Cohesive teams socialize and spend time together away from the office. Although it is difficult to force cohesiveness, you can encourage it by interacting often with other people in your team. Researchers found that cohesive teams share the five characteristics shown in Figure A-8.

4. Request information

In most organizations information is power and the fuel used to make key decisions. High-performing teams usually know the company's strategy, financial condition, future direction, and upcoming changes. When your team learns new information, you can clarify your goals and revise your tasks as necessary.

5. Recognize team contributions

QUICK TIP

Be careful not to discourage other people by praising only the high performers.

A high-performing team recognizes that it is making important contributions to the company. Knowing you are part of a highly successful group is usually a source of motivation to keep working and excel. During team meetings, mention one or two accomplishments of the team to recognize your contributions. Being a member of a successful team has a lot of benefits. See Figure A-9.

YOU TRY IT

1. Use a word processor such as Microsoft Office Word to open the file A-6.doc provided with your Data Files, and save it as Perform.doc in the location where you store your Data Files

2. Read the contents of Perform.doc, which describe a business team

3. List the characteristics of the team, and identify whether it is a high-performing team

4. Save and close Perform.doc, then submit it to your instructor as requested

FIGURE A-8: Characteristics of cohesive teams

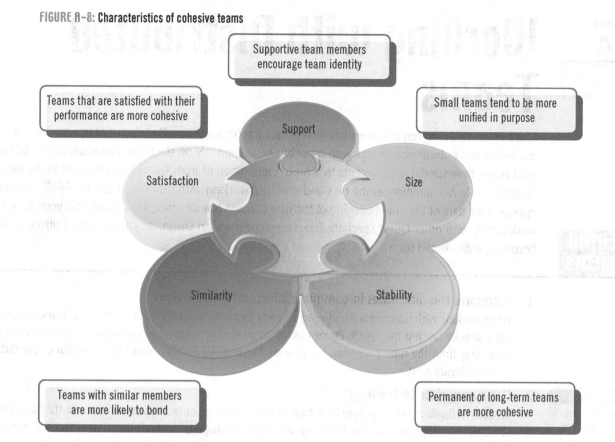

Supportive team members encourage team identity

Teams that are satisfied with their performance are more cohesive

Small teams tend to be more unified in purpose

Support

Satisfaction

Size

Similarity

Stability

Teams with similar members are more likely to bond

Permanent or long-term teams are more cohesive

Source: Beal, D. J., et al, "Cohesion and performance in groups: A meta-analytic clarification of construct relations," *Journal of Applied Psychology*, 2003.

FIGURE A-9: Benefits of being a member of a successful team

Helps to overcome obstacles and solve problems

Reduces stress and promotes physical well-being

Encourages active participation, which leads to additional success

Produces greater satisfaction, self-confidence, and self-esteem

© Jupiterimages Corporation

Teamwork

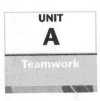

Working with Distributed Teams

A **distributed team** has members in different geographic locations. Distributed teams are becoming more common as businesses merge with other businesses and rely on electronic communication. Distributed teams have special requirements that make them different from teams that can meet in the same location. Table A-5 summarizes the do's and don'ts of working with distributed teams. As you approach the date of the grand opening of the new Chicago branch office, Don Novak asks your team to work closely with other Quest Specialty Travel employees in San Diego. As you do, you realize you are becoming a distributed team.

ESSENTIAL ELEMENTS

1. Recognize the difficulties in communication and coordination

When working with teammates who live in different locations, be aware of the difficulties. Team members can communicate less frequently. Phone calls often need to be scheduled in advance. Differences in time zones may limit the time your team has to work together. Distributed teams need to balance the skills shown in Figure A-10.

> **QUICK TIP**
> Wikis are becoming popular tools for distributed groups to share information.

2. Use appropriate technology

Modern technology allows people to remain in near-constant contact regardless of where they are. Take advantage of cell phones, fax machines, e-mail, instant messaging, file sharing, and conferencing software to keep in touch.

3. Attend occasional face-to-face meetings

Although technology makes it easier to communicate with distributed team members, talking face to face builds team unity. Look for chances to physically meet with other people on your team. Businesses often arrange kickoff meetings and follow-up meetings for distributed teams. Otherwise, take advantage of conferences, training sessions, and company meetings, for example. Occasional meetings between individual team members can strengthen the team overall.

4. Use a coordinator

On a distributed team, someone needs to spend time coordinating team activities and keeping members informed. If possible, serve as or suggest a coordinator or **proxy** who regularly contacts everyone, develops and manages the team's calendar, distributes information, and collects needed information and reports.

5. Set and attend regular activities

A successful distributed team meets regularly, such as once a week during a conference call. During times of high activity, you can discuss the details of your tasks and set priorities. During times of low activity, you can still check in, talk about goals, and maintain a connection with other team members.

YOU TRY IT

1. Use a word processor such as Microsoft Office Word to open the file A-7.doc provided with your Data Files, and save it as Distributed.doc in the location where you store your Data Files

2. Read the contents of Distributed.doc, which describe a team that has members in three countries

3. Suggest how the team can work together more effectively

4. Save and close Distributed.doc, then submit it to your instructor as requested

FIGURE A-10: Skills distributed teams need

Manage projects	Manage yourself
Network with others	Be aware of cultural differences
Use technology	Be aware of interpersonal differences

TABLE A-5: Working with distributed teams do's and don'ts

guideline	do	don't
Recognize the difficulties	Acknowledge that differences in location can create obstacles	**Don't** expect a distributed team to work the same way a traditional team does
Use technology	• Take advantage of cell phones, e-mail, instant messaging, and other technology to stay in touch with teammates • Use conferencing software to meet online	**Don't** overlook business etiquette when using e-mail and instant messages
Attend face-to-face meetings	• Look for chances to physically meet with team members • Take advantage of conferences, training sessions, and other opportunities	**Don't** rely solely on technology—meet team members in person when you can
Coordinate regular activities	• Serve as the team coordinator or suggest someone who can • Set up regular events such as weekly phone calls • Use team time to solve problems, verify tasks, and set priorities	**Don't** skip regular team activities when you are busy

Fun and games get serious

Three-dimensional virtual worlds are online applications that let users interact with one another and create and use objects. Most of these applications started as games, including the popular Second Life (see the "Technology @ Work" lesson). Recently, established technology companies such as IBM, Sun Microsystems, and Nortel have introduced virtual world applications for business. "It's the next evolution of the Internet – the 3D Web," says David Wortley, director of the Serious Games Institute. Virtual worlds are especially suited to training for emergencies. Fire drills and disaster planning can only go so far. In a virtual world, you can simulate a disaster such as a hurricane or flood, and then record the responses. An entire company can learn from the simulated event and from their mistakes, which don't have real consequences in a virtual world.
Sources: Au, Wagner James, "Enterprise Virtual Worlds to See Real-World Growth," GigaOm Web site, *http://gigaom.com*, October 6, 2009; Swabey, Pete, "Serious Business in Virtual Worlds," *Information-Age*, October 19, 2007.

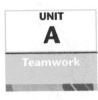
Technology @ Work: Virtual Worlds

Distributed groups can use virtual worlds to interact and keep in touch. A **virtual world** is a simulated world that you can explore, manipulate, and affect. One of the most popular virtual worlds is Second Life (*http://secondlife.com*). Businesses are using virtual worlds to train employees, simulate business processes, and host events. For distributed groups with members in different locations and time zones, a virtual world lets participants network and collaborate realistically by conversing, gesturing, and exchanging objects. For example, companies use Second Life to create virtual workplaces where employees can meet, communicate with each other, teach one another skills, and trade information. Now that your team in Chicago is working closely with the Quest Specialty Travel main office in San Diego, Don Novak suggests you learn how to use Second Life for team interactions.

ESSENTIAL ELEMENTS

1. **Create an account and move around**

    Visit the main page of Second Life to create a free account. After you create a user name and password and select a starting look for your avatar, you can select a location to explore. (An avatar is your online character.) Next, you download and install the software you need from Second Life, and then you can explore the virtual world, using the keyboard to control your movements. Second Life provides a tutorial to help you get acquainted. See Figure A-11.

    QUICK TIP
    In general, greet people as you enter and leave a location in Second Life.

2. **Interact with other residents**

    As you move around and explore, you will meet other Second Life residents. You can have open, public chats with them or private conversations using Second Life's instant messaging feature. To meet with coworkers, you can arrange a meeting place. As with other social media sites, you can create a list of friends so you know when they are online in Second Life.

    QUICK TIP
    No other technology lets distributed teams simulate how to prepare for emergencies.

3. **Form groups and have meetings**

    To meet people on your work team, you can create and join a group. After you feel comfortable in the Second Life world, you can create a work space for yourself and your team. You can do so in the main Second Life site, or use Second Life Work, which is an associated, secure site designed for businesses who want to have virtual meetings.

    For example, IBM and Intel have used Second Life for major conferences with speakers and attendees from around the world. Figure A-12 shows the virtual workplace the National Oceanic and Atmospheric Administration's (NOAA) created in Second Life, a place called Meteora Island. Residents can attend conferences where the NOAA simulates events such as tsunamis and hurricanes.

YOU TRY IT

1. Open a Web browser such as Microsoft Internet Explorer or Mozilla Firefox, and go to the Second Life main page at *http://secondlife.com*

2. Follow the on-screen instructions to create an account, download and install the software, and then enter a Second Life location

3. Use the tutorial to learn how to explore the Second Life world

4. Click the Search button, type Meteora Island in the Search box, press Enter, and then click the Teleport button to visit Meteora Island

5. Take a screen shot of your avatar on Meteora Island and send it to your instructor

FIGURE A-11: Tutorial in Second Life

Click to start
the tutorial

Movement
controls

Type chat text
in the Local
Chat box

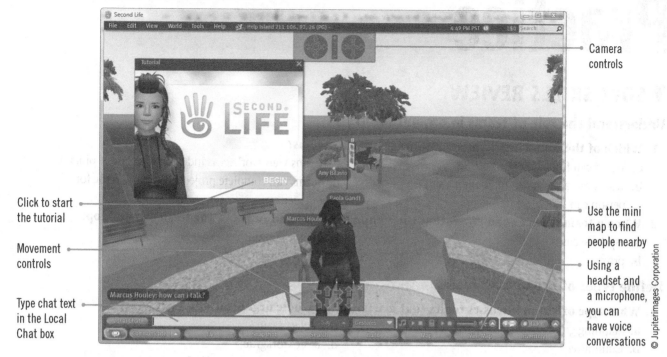

Camera
controls

Use the mini
map to find
people nearby

Using a
headset and
a microphone,
you can
have voice
conversations

© Jupiterimages Corporation

FIGURE A-12: NOAA's Meteora Island

© Jupiterimages Corporation

Practice

▼ SOFT SKILLS REVIEW

Understand the role of teams in organizations.

1. Which of the following is *not* an advantage of using teams?
   a. Teams can find creative solutions
   b. Teams can accomplish more than a single person can
   c. Teams view workers as independent sources of labor
   d. Teams can complete projects that are too big for one person

2. When a team is part of an effort that the company values and respects, the team can develop:
   a. esprit de corps
   b. proxy
   c. ad hoc committees
   d. quality circles

Define types of groups and teams.

1. What type of group discusses topics that matter to the whole organization?
   a. Standing group
   b. Committee
   c. Project team
   d. Basic workgroup

2. Groups of workers who identify and solve work-related problems are called:
   a. committees
   b. ad hoc groups
   c. task forces
   d. quality circles

Recognize differences between groups and teams.

1. A number of people who work on similar tasks or follow the same procedures is called a:
   a. team
   b. distribution
   c. self-managed trust
   d. group

2. If a group focuses on individual tasks and responsibilities, what does a team focus on?
   a. Individual goals and processes
   b. Team accomplishments
   c. Shared tasks and responsibilities
   d. Decisions that affect each member

Ensure team success.

1. Which of the following is *not* a common role on a well-functioning team?
   a. Creative thinker
   b. Specialist
   c. Detail recorder
   d. Humanist

2. On successful teams, who typically sets the team goals?
   a. Managers
   b. Team members
   c. Only the team leader
   d. The team member in the goal-setter role

Empower teams.

1. Which of the following is *not* a typical reason that organizations form teams?
   a. To produce something
   b. To create necessary work
   c. To generate ideas
   d. To solve problems

2. Before you join a team, you should:
   a. set goals for the team
   b. make sure your individual projects are completed
   c. decide which role you will play
   d. talk to a decision maker about the purpose of the team

Earn rewards for team effort.

1. Which of the following is a way you can promote your team?
   a. Praise team accomplishments
   b. Accept easy tasks that fit your job description
   c. Emphasize individual successes
   d. Praise your manager

2. Before an employee review, many companies ask the employee to complete a(n):

a. supervisor appraisal form   c. team evaluation form

b. self-evaluation form   d. disclosure form

Become a high-performing team.

1. High-performing teams are cohesive. This means that team members:

a. avoid socializing outside of work   c. work closely together

b. are more different than similar   d. work in different locations

2. Which of the following is *not* a characteristic of a high-performing team?

a. Stability   c. Satisfaction

b. Support   d. Strictness

Work with distributed teams.

1. A distributed team has:

a. members in different geographic locations   c. long-term members

b. extra cohesiveness   d. many contacts in the organization

2. Which of the following is a typical problem for distributed teams?

a. Lack of cooperation   c. Difficulty finding technology

b. Difficulty meeting   d. Low performance

Technology @ Work: Virtual worlds

1. What is a virtual world?

a. An undiscovered world   c. A simulated world that you can explore, manipulate, and affect

b. A place designed for businesses to exchange goods and services   d. A place that demands your best behavior

2. One secure site designed for businesses that want to have virtual meetings is called:

a. Second Life Work   c. First Life

b. Second Life Secure   d. After Work

▼ CRITICAL THINKING QUESTIONS

1. This unit describes the roles that people can play in a team. Which role do you often take in a group or team? Which role do you often avoid? Explain why.

2. As mentioned in the introduction to this unit, not all teams are effective. In fact, as many as 9 out of 10 teams are ineffective, meaning they fail to complete their assigned tasks. What can make a team ineffective?

3. Think about the most cohesive group or team you have been a part of. How did it feel to be part of that team? How much time did you spend with other members? What was it about that group that made it cohesive?

4. Comparing the definitions of groups and teams makes teams seem more desirable. In what situations might a team be less desirable or effective than a group?

5. Have you been a member of a distributed team? Describe the pros and cons of working on such a team.

▼ INDEPENDENT CHALLENGE 1

You are an administrative assistant at Newberry Heating & Cooling, a contracting company in Columbus, Ohio. Your supervisor, Joanne Burton, has heard that groups and teams can complete more tasks than people working on their own. She asks you to find out what types of teams businesses can have, and then to describe each type. During the next staff meeting, she wants to present the list and discuss which type would be the best for the administrative assistants. She has already started the list and asks you to complete it. See Figure A-13.

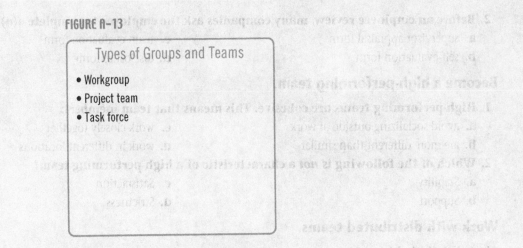

Types of Groups and Teams

- Workgroup
- Project team
- Task force

a. Use word-processing software such as Microsoft Office Word to open the file **A-8.doc** provided with your Data Files, and save it as **Team Types.doc** in the location where you store your Data Files.

b. Complete the list of group and team types, and then add descriptions of each type.

c. Submit the document to your instructor as requested.

▼ INDEPENDENT CHALLENGE 2

PT at Home is a small and growing business in Syracuse, New York. George Lambert founded the company a few years ago to provide physical therapy services to people in their homes. You work as a coordinator, helping to schedule clients and home therapy sessions. George wants to assemble a team for a new project—working with health clubs to provide physical therapy to its members. George asks you to help him assign the right people to the team. He has created a diagram of the roles he wants each team member to play. See Figure A-14.

FIGURE A-14

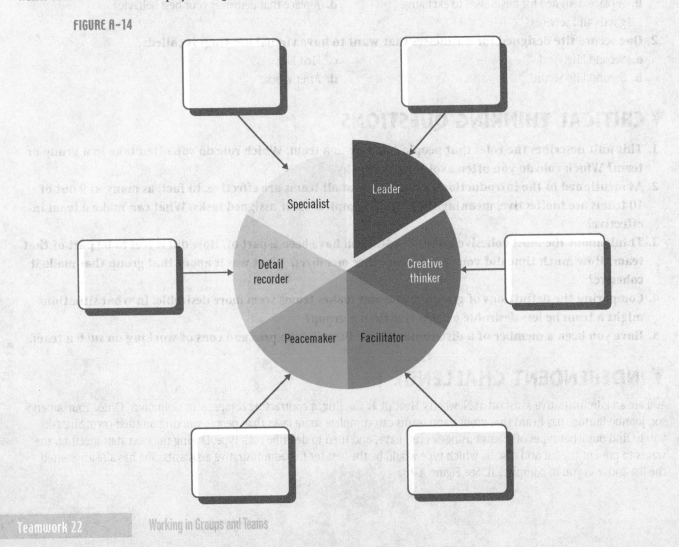

a. Use word-processing software such as Microsoft Office Word to open the file **A-9.doc** provided with your Data Files, and save it as **Team Roles.doc** in the location where you store your Data Files.

b. Use presentation software such as Microsoft Office PowerPoint to open the file **A-10.pptx** provided with your Data Files, and save it as **Project Team.pptx** in the location where you store your Data Files.

c. Read the descriptions of the PT at Home employees in Team Roles.doc. Based on those descriptions, assign each employee to a team role in the Project Team.pptx presentation.

d. Submit the document and presentation to your instructor as requested.

▼ REAL LIFE INDEPENDENT CHALLENGE

Whether you are a member of a group or team at work or not, you can develop your group skills online. Reading job blogs, contributing comments, and joining online groups can build your communication skills and knowledge about getting along in the current working world. CareerBuilder.com recommends the following job blogs for people who are working or looking for a job:

- Brazen Careerist: *http://blog.penelopetrunk.com*
- Career Diva: *www.evetahmincioglu.com/web/blog*
- CareerRealism: *www.careerealism.com*
- Evil HR Lady: *http://evilhrlady.blogspot.com*
- On the Job: *www.45things.com/blog.php*
- On Careers: *www.usnews.com/money/blogs/outside-voices-careers*
- Personal Branding: *www.personalbrandingblog.com*

a. Visit three or four of the job blogs listed in this exercise.

b. On the current main page, look for topics that interest you. Also look for categories of topics that earlier posts have covered. Look for articles and categories related to working on groups and teams.

c. When you find an article that offers advice you can use, save the article as a Favorite. (In Internet Explorer, click the Favorites button on the Command bar, and then click Add to Favorites.)

▼ TEAM CHALLENGE

You are working for Peachtree Landscapers, a landscaping company in Atlanta, Georgia. The company specializes in creating natural landscapes for business and residential customers. They emphasize environmentally friendly practices and ecological landscapes. You are a new employee at Peachtree Landscapes, working as an assistant office manager. Liz Montoya, the owner of Peachtree Landscapes, wants all the employees to work together as a team. During each staff meeting, she wants to spend some time doing team-building exercises. For your first meeting, Liz has planned an icebreaker exercise designed to build common bonds.

a. Working with your group, introduce yourself to each person in the group.

b. Mention one place you've visited recently that you enjoyed. This can be a city, area of your town, building, or spot in the woods. In a sentence or two, explain what you enjoyed about this place.

c. Next, identify a person you admire. This can be someone everyone knows or a personal acquaintance. (For personal acquaintances, use first names only.)

d. After all of the introductions, mention one thing you have in common with each person in the group.

▼ BE THE CRITIC

You have been working for the Oregon Inn, a midsized hotel in downtown Salem, Oregon, for a few months. The Oregon Inn has four other locations in Oregon and Washington. Jay Schuster, the manager of your hotel, has been trying to create an effective team of 20 employees from all the Oregon Inns. So far, the team has met once in person. Figure A-15 lists the activities the team performed at the meeting. Analyze these activities, and then create a list of their strengths and weaknesses. Send the list to your instructor as requested.

FIGURE A-15

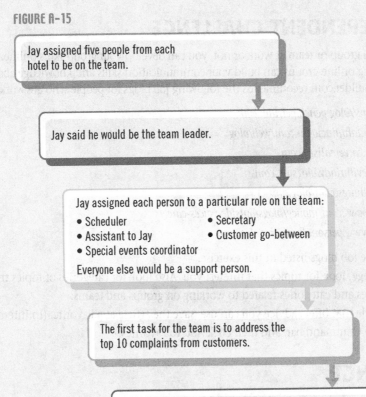

Jay assigned five people from each hotel to be on the team.

Jay said he would be the team leader.

Jay assigned each person to a particular role on the team:
- Scheduler
- Assistant to Jay
- Special events coordinator
- Secretary
- Customer go-between

Everyone else would be a support person.

The first task for the team is to address the top 10 complaints from customers.

Jay said he has an urgent deadline—the task must be completed by next week for a confidential reason.

Exploring Team Roles and Processes

Before a team can develop into an effective unit, members need to assume certain roles. A role is a set of behaviors. For example, the team member in the leader role organizes team meetings and creates the agenda. Each role should contribute to the team's success. Teams need time to explore, identify, and assume roles. During this time, teams typically pass through clearly defined stages as they progress from a group to a team. In this unit you will learn about the most common types of team roles, the group development process, and practical advice for establishing an effective work environment for teams. You are working as assistant office manager for the Quest Specialty Travel branch office in Chicago, Illinois. As the head of the branch, Don Novak has assigned you and other members of the Quest staff to a team in charge of the grand opening of the office. He is now encouraging your team to accept roles and outline how you will work together.

OBJECTIVES

Map the stages of group development

Recognize the need for team leadership

Select team members

Choose the optimal team size

Define common team roles

Establish team rules

Clarify team objectives

Make collective decisions

Mapping the Stages of Group Development

Before a group can address new challenges, develop effective solutions, and deliver results, it must evolve into a unified team. Bruce Tuckman, an American psychologist studying group dynamics, described the development from group to team as Forming – Storming – Norming – Performing. See Figure B-1. Other models of group development are similar. Table B-1 summarizes the activities and characteristics of a group as it completes each stage of the process. Now that Don has selected members of the Quest Chicago branch office team, he suggests you learn about the stages of group development.

DETAILS

A group passes through the following stages when developing into a team:

- **Forming**

  One of the first steps in team building is to form the group. People are selected or volunteer to join the group. They meet to learn about their new responsibilities. At this point, members of the group behave politely, but still work independently. They need time to get to know one another, share their backgrounds, and start forming relationships. Team leaders should avoid working on major tasks during this stage.

QUICK TIP

Some groups move through this stage quickly. If the group has incompatible members, the group might never pass this stage.

- **Storming**

  As the team's responsibilities become clearer, people compete to promote their ideas and establish their positions in the group. At the same time, the group talks about their shared objectives, defines the process for working together, and debates the rules they will follow. Conflict is a normal part of this stage.

- **Norming**

  If the group can resolve conflicts in the storming stage, it can enter the norming stage and begin working as a team. Members agree on how they will behave and work together. They begin to understand and trust each other. At this point, the team leader can assign more tasks and responsibilities to members. This stage is called norming because the group adopts **norms**—the rules it uses for appropriate and inappropriate values, beliefs, attitudes, and behaviors.

- **Performing**

  Groups that reach the performing stage have evolved into effective teams. During this stage, a team accomplishes most of its significant work. Team members work together as a unit, complete tasks smoothly, and require little supervision. Team members depend on one another and see themselves as part of a larger whole. They might still have conflicts, but they usually resolve them constructively. At this point, the leader should focus on providing direction and motivation.

- **Transforming**

  Occasionally, a team with the right mix of people comes together and performs in extraordinary ways. When a group develops close relationships and a strong sense of unity, it can transform into a high-performing team. This phase is not automatic, and most groups do not evolve to this level.

- **Adjourning**

  After a team accomplishes its assigned tasks, it needs to be dissolved. This adjourning stage usually happens after the performing stage, but can happen during or after the transforming stage. Some teams resist breaking up and try to continue working as a team. If a business has other suitable tasks for the team, it might take advantage of the team's maturity and allow it to continue. Other teams, such as committees, are standing groups that replace members with new participants. When new members join a team, it completes the adjourning stage and returns to the storming stage to redefine itself, as shown in Figure B-1.

FIGURE B-1: Stages of group development

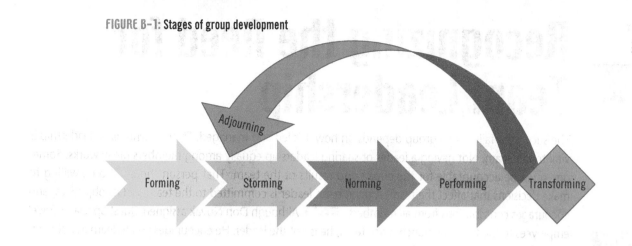

Forming → Storming → Norming → Performing → Transforming

Adjourning

TABLE B-1: Activities and characteristics of each stage

stage	activities	characteristics
Forming	• Get acquainted • Share backgrounds • Discuss purpose of the team • Identify information to gather	• Most members are optimistic • Some members might be impatient to work on tasks
Storming	• Define tasks • Rank tasks • Discuss objectives and the process for working together	• Members have competing points of view • Conflict and tension are normal • Attitudes toward the group change frequently
Norming	• Agree on how to behave and work together • Cooperate on assigned tasks	• Members are enthusiastic about the focus of the team • Members enjoy unity and team spirit
Performing	• Recognize and solve problems • Make changes • Accomplish tasks and reach goals	• Members are closely attached to the team • Team understands and appreciates its strengths and weaknesses
Transforming	• Work as a unit • Perform above expectations	Members share a sense that they are part of something special
Adjourning	• Complete the final tasks • Review accomplishments • Disband or reform to work on a new set of goals • Share improved process with others	Members are reluctant to leave the team

Other models of group development

Besides Bruce Tuckman, other people have described how groups develop into teams. For example, George Charrier, an employee of Procter & Gamble, said a small group of people must complete five stages to work efficiently. Together, he called the stages Cog's Ladder. The stages are the *polite stage*, the *why we're here stage*, the *power stage*, the *cooperation stage* and the *esprit stage*. As in the Forming – Storming – Norming – Performing stages, groups can only move forward after completing the current stage. Marshall Scott Poole took a different point of view. Instead of following certain stages, Poole said that groups work on three types of goals, or tracks, at the same time.

In the *task track*, the group focuses on meeting its goals. In the *relation track*, group members work on their relationships with each other. For example, while working on tasks, team members might share personal information or exchange jokes. In the *topic track*, the group discusses problems and concerns. When a group switches from one track to another, such as shifting from joking to solving a problem during a meeting, Poole calls that a *breakpoint*.

Source: "Group Development," Wikipedia Web site, *http://en.wikipedia.org/wiki/Group_development*, accessed January 22, 2010.

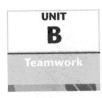

Recognizing the Need for Team Leadership

The success or failure of a group depends on how it is led and managed. Strong, centralized leadership is vital to any team. Not having a leader or sharing leadership equally among members rarely works. Someone must be accountable for the efforts and results of the team. That person should also be willing to make decisions that affect the team. A good team leader is committed to the team and its objectives, and encourages contributions from all members. Although Don Novak assigned Quest Specialty Travel employees to the Chicago branch office team, he is not the leader. He encourages you to learn about team leadership so the group can select a leader.

ESSENTIAL ELEMENTS

1. ### Assign or elect a leader
   The manager who formed the group might assign someone to oversee the group's efforts. In other cases, the team defines or selects its own leader. Team members tend to be more responsive to a leader they elect. An informal leader can emerge when the formal leader is not effective or does not have the full support of the group's members. Figure B-2 defines leadership and formal and informal leaders.

2. ### Participate in team assignments
   Effective teams are made up of people who work closely together. The team leader should be a participating member of the group so he or she can work closely with other members. The leader should also be responsible for tasks and work with others on shared assignments. Members have more respect for someone who can lead by example, not from behind a desk.

> **QUICK TIP**
> A team leader occasionally communicates with management on the team's behalf to clear obstacles that might hurt or hinder the team.

3. ### Communicate with management
   A team leader is the liaison to the organization's management. (A **liaison** is a person who relays information between groups.) An effective leader has a reputation for accomplishing tasks. He or she also maintains good relationships with key stakeholders in the company. The leader should clearly communicate the team's purpose, goals, and methods to others in the company.

4. ### Serve as team motivator
   Successful teams share a vision about the team's purpose that excites all the members. Effective team leaders motivate their teams to accomplish goals. Leaders are also committed to the team and their tasks. Team leaders often have the traits shown in Figure B-3.

> **QUICK TIP**
> Leaders drawn from the ranks of a team often have trouble managing conflict among peers.

5. ### Manage conflict
   Team leaders should recognize and manage the conflicts that are inevitable in a team. A person that prefers to avoid conflict can be harmful to a group's development if problems fester or expand when they are not addressed.

YOU TRY IT

1. **Use a word processor such as Microsoft Office Word to open the file B-1.doc provided with your Data Files, and save it as Leadership.doc in the location where you store your Data Files**

2. **Read the contents of Leadership.doc, which describe a team looking for a leader**

3. **Identify each group member's strengths and weaknesses as a leader**

4. **Save and close Leadership.doc, then submit it to your instructor as requested**

Leadership means influencing others to achieve a goal

Formal leaders hold a position of authority, which they use to influence others

Informal leaders do not have a formal position of authority but share traits of an effective leader

© Jupiterimages Corporation

FIGURE B-3: Traits of a team leader

Open	Conscientious	Extraverted	Agreeable	Confident
Curious	Organized	Outgoing	Tolerant	Self-assured
Original	Punctual	Talkative	Sensitive	Optimistic
Creative	Dependable	Sociable	Trusting	Encouraging

Selecting Team Members

One of the first challenges a team leader faces is how to assemble a group of people that will evolve into a winning team. Some managers select team members for the leader. In other cases, the leader follows a process similar to hiring a new employee. If you are serving as team leader, your goal is to select current employees that can contribute the most to your team's objectives. The quality of the people you select determines the quality of the team's efforts and results. Table B-2 summarizes the do's and don'ts of selecting team members.  Because you have worked for Quest Specialty Travel longer than any other member of the Quest Chicago branch office team, the group elects you as the team leader. Now you need to reduce the size of the team by selecting only necessary members.

ESSENTIAL ELEMENTS

QUICK TIP

Ask yourself *what* sort of people you need on the team before you ask *who.*

1. Understand the demands of the project or assignment

Team members who are selected on the basis of friendship, familiarity, or loyalty are often not those best suited for the job. Select members based on the characteristics of the project and the team's assigned objectives.

2. Carefully consider attitude

Many managers say that a person's attitude is the most important characteristic to consider when making team selections. Team members with positive attitudes tend to work harder, meet goals, and cooperate with others. People with negative attitudes are more likely to be unmotivated and self-absorbed, which creates problems for the team.

QUICK TIP

Skills and attitude are tightly related. Don't recruit a skilled person who has a poor attitude.

3. Secure needed skills

Most team projects require particular skills. These skills range from Web design to creative writing. As you begin planning for your team and understanding the demands of the project, list specialized skills you need. Then recruit someone who has those talents. However, avoid the mistake of selecting mediocre workers to join the team because they have skills you need. Figure B-4 illustrates the relationship between attitude and skills.

4. Create a broad knowledge base

Each member of the team contributes their unique knowledge, work history, experience, and ideas. The team can draw on all of this knowledge as the project unfolds. As you select team members, give careful thought to the knowledge that different people could offer the team. Don't overlook untraditional knowledge, such as a long history with the company or experience with a competitor.

5. Beware of animosities

As you narrow your selections, consider how each candidate fits into the team. Would he or she work well with the other members? Do others in the organization have high regards for the candidate? Does the candidate have the time and attention to devote to the team effort? Does the candidate have personality conflicts, or animosities, with someone else?

YOU TRY IT

1. Use a word processor such as Microsoft Office Word to open the file B-2.doc provided with your Data Files, and save it as Selections.doc in the location where you store your Data Files

2. Read the contents of Selections.doc, which describe potential team members

3. Select members of the team to meet the objectives described in Selections.doc

4. Save and close Selections.doc, then submit it to your instructor as requested

FIGURE B-4: Relationship between attitude and skills

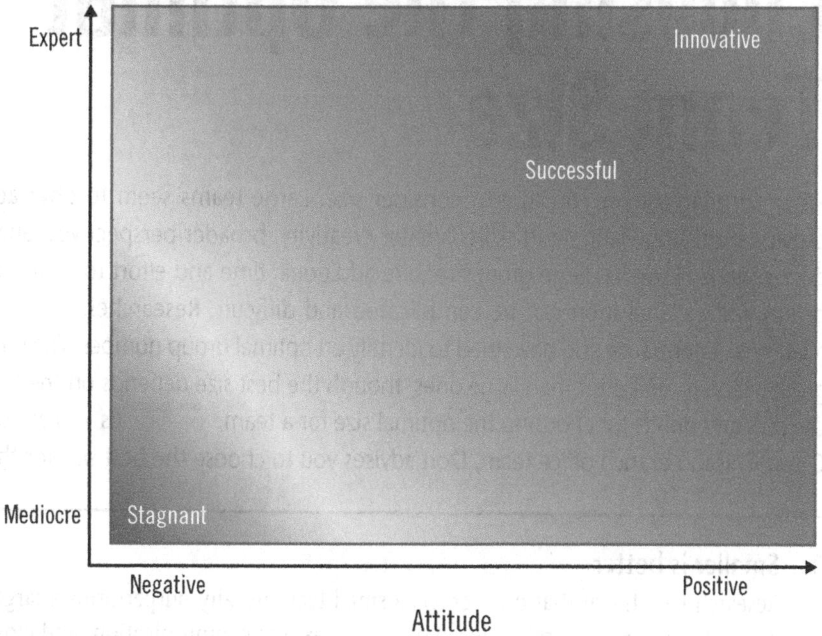

Choose team members based on their attitude and skills. Successful teams have members with excellent skills and positive attitudes. Teams that do not accomplish their goals are stagnant due to mediocre skills and negative attitudes. Innovative teams are unusual. Their members have expert skills and very positive attitudes.

TABLE B-2: Selecting team members do's and don'ts

guideline	do	don't
Understand the demands of the project	Select members that fit the characteristics of the project and the objectives	**Don't** select members based on friendship, familiarity, or loyalty
Consider attitude	Select members with positive attitudes about the team assignments	**Don't** select members with negative attitudes and hope they improve
Secure needed skills	• List specialized skills your team requires • Recruit team members who have the skills you need • Make sure you can replace weak performers	**Don't** select mediocre workers only because they have some skills you need
Create a broad knowledge base	Recognize the unique knowledge and experience that each team member can contribute	**Don't** overlook untraditional knowledge, such as experience with a competitor
Beware of animosities	• Consider how each candidate fits into the team • Select people who would work well with other team members	**Don't** select someone who might have a personality conflict with another team member

Dream teams often fail

One of the first so-called dream teams was the 2004 United States Olympic basketball team. This dream team contained only NBA stars. Sports fans expected it to easily win a gold medal. Instead, it finished third and lost to Lithuania. In fact, according to Geoffrey Colvin at *Fortune* magazine, most dream teams fail because they're "bunches of people," not teams. As contrast, Colvin relates the story of assembling the 1980 U.S. Olympic hockey team. "Coach Herb Brooks . . . based his picks on personal chemistry. In the story's movie version, 'Miracle,' Brooks' assistant looks at the roster and objects that many of the country's greatest college players were left out (professionals were not eligible to play then). To which Brooks responds with this essential anti-dream-team philosophy: 'I'm not lookin' for the best players, Craig. I'm lookin' for the right players.'" Colvin claims that "signing too many all-stars" usually leads to team failure. Instead, he provides the business example of Worthington Industries, a steel-processing company in Ohio. "When an employee is hired to join a plant-floor team, he works for a 90-day probationary period, after which the team votes to determine whether he can stay." Worthington's CEO, John McConnell, explains. "Give us people who are dedicated to making the team work, as opposed to a bunch of talented people with big egos, and we'll win every time."

Source: Colvin, Geoffrey, "Why Dream Teams Fail," *Fortune*, June 1, 2006.

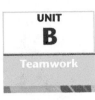

UNIT
B
Teamwork

Choosing the Optimal Team Size

When forming a team, be sure to consider size. Large teams seem to offer advantages. More people provide more knowledge and skills, greater creativity, broader perspectives, and more hands to actually do the work. However, large groups require additional time and effort to coordinate activities. Communication and collaboration can be complicated and difficult. Researchers have examined team size as it relates to performance and have tried to identify an optimal group number. Their findings suggest that small groups tend to do better than large ones, though the best size depends on the team's goals. Table B-3 lists the do's and don'ts for choosing the optimal size for a team. As you are selecting members for the Quest Chicago branch office team, Don advises you to choose the best size for the team.

ESSENTIAL ELEMENTS

1. **Smaller is better**

   Research has shown that on average, a small team usually outperforms a large one. Better performance comes from a small team's reduced overhead, ease of communication, and close relationships. Although there is no magic number for team size, studies suggest that the ideal size for most groups is between 5 and 10 participants. Small groups allow each member to participate actively. See Figure B-5.

   QUICK TIP
   Air time is the amount of time available for someone to speak to the group.

2. **Size affects communication**

   As a group grows, more people need to communicate with each other. Team size can be a problem if too many people are competing for air time during a meeting or e-mail in-boxes become congested with messages from team members. When teams grow larger than 12 people, interaction becomes more difficult.

   QUICK TIP
   If a large committee needs to actively work on a task, it usually organizes a smaller subcommittee.

3. **Deliberative groups can have many members**

   A **deliberative group** discusses or debates a topic, such as a committee that creates company policies. Committees and information-sharing groups can work effectively even if they have more members than traditional work groups. These types of teams perform few tasks. Instead, they discuss a problem or other topic until they reach a conclusion.

   QUICK TIP
   If a virtual team has poor communication support, a large group size will quickly choke it.

4. **Virtual teams can be large**

   Virtual teams include members who do not work in a common location. They typically complete tasks more slowly than other teams because they are not physically located in the same place. If people can connect to one another easily, these distributed groups can be as large as 20–25 members. After that, participants tend to lose focus or split into factions.

5. **Quick-response teams are very small**

   Some teams are assigned to projects that demand quick solutions. In these cases, a group of three empowered people are more responsive and successful than even a slightly larger team. Speed favors a group that can meet and make decisions as necessary.

YOU TRY IT

1. Use a word processor such as Microsoft Office Word to open the file B-3.doc provided with your Data Files, and save it as Team Size.doc in the location where you store your Data Files

2. Read the contents of Team Size.doc, which describe a team

3. Identify how many members the team should have

4. Save and close Team Size.doc, then submit it to your instructor as requested

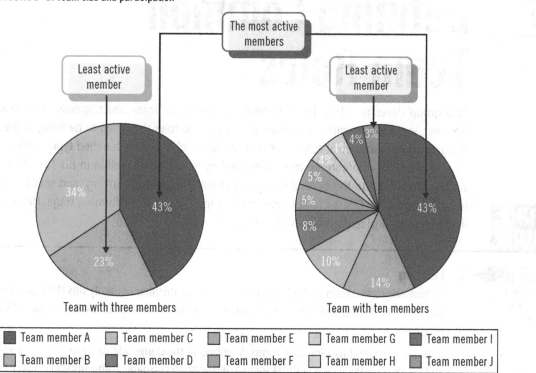

FIGURE B-5: Team size and participation

The most active members

Least active member

Least active member

34%

43%

23%

Team with three members

4% 3%
4%
4%
5%
5%
8%
10%
14%
43%

Team with ten members

| ■ Team member A | □ Team member C | ■ Team member E | □ Team member G | ■ Team member I |
| ■ Team member B | ■ Team member D | ■ Team member F | □ Team member H | ■ Team member J |

Whether a team is large or small, the most active member speaks 43% of the time. In a small team of three members, the least active member participates 23% of the time. In a larger team of 10 members, the least active member participates only 3% of the time.

Source: McGrath, J. E. (1984). *Groups: Interaction and performance.* Englewood Cliffs, NJ: Prentice Hall.

TABLE B-3: Choosing the optimal team size do's and don'ts

guideline	do	don't
Smaller is better	• Choose 5–10 members for a team, depending on its goals • For a team that needs to make quick decisions, limit members to three	**Don't** make the mistake of assuming that largegroups can complete more tasks
Size affects communication	Make sure the people in a team can communicate with each other easily	**Don't** select more than 12 people for a project team or other group that needs to interact easily
Specialty groups can be larger	• Allow deliberative groups to have many members • Make sure members of virtual teams can connect to each other easily • Allow virtual teams to have up to 25 members	**Don't** expect virtual teams to work quickly **Don't** organize virtual groups of more than 25 members—they tend to lose focus or split into factions

Defining Common Team Roles

As a group develops into a team, it needs to clarify the roles and responsibilities of each member. However, individual members are often unaware of the roles that need to be filled, or are only comfortable managing responsibilities familiar to them. Researchers have identified typical roles that teams use. Among the most common are those identified by Raymond M. Belbin in his 1981 book *Management Teams*, which fall into the general categories of leading, doing, thinking, and socializing. Don Novak sees that the Quest Chicago branch office team is still in the forming stage. He encourages you to define the roles and responsibilities of your team.

ESSENTIAL ELEMENTS

QUICK TIP
Belbin called *leading* and *doing* action-oriented roles.

1. **Leading**

   At least one formal team leader is required. This group member naturally fills the leading role. Other team members can also support the leader by helping to motivate and direct the team, especially in large teams.

2. **Doing**

   This is the broadest role for most teams. Members in the doing role take most of the team responsibilities and complete tasks. Types of doers include implementers, shapers, and finishers. These types are further described in Figure B-6.

QUICK TIP
Specialists play cerebral roles, which focus on thinking and problem solving.

3. **Thinking**

   This includes people that have a talent for design, creativity, and problem solving. Some teams also require **specialists**, people with particular talents or abilities that are relevant to the assigned tasks.

QUICK TIP
Belbin called *socializing* a people-oriented role.

4. **Socializing**

   This role is best served by people with strong interpersonal skills who can help to coordinate, motivate, and build the team. These people support and encourage relationships and interaction among members. There is often a need for people who can also reach beyond the group's boundaries and work with other decision makers and stakeholders to further the team's efforts.

5. **Determining roles**

   Roles usually emerge through one or more of the following factors: Management expectations or assignments; demands of the job, project, or client; training or education; and affinity, which is a natural attraction to certain tasks. Table B-4 further describes how a group can assign these roles.

YOU TRY IT

1. Use a word processor such as Microsoft Office Word to open the file B-4.doc provided with your Data Files, and save it as Roles.doc in the location where you store your Data Files

2. Read the contents of Roles.doc, which describe team members

3. Assign a role to each group member

4. Save and close Roles.doc, then submit it to your instructor as requested

FIGURE B-6: Types of group members in the *doing* role

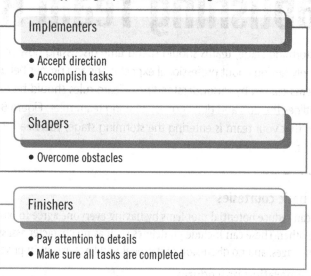

Implementers
- Accept direction
- Accomplish tasks

Shapers
- Overcome obstacles

Finishers
- Pay attention to details
- Make sure all tasks are completed

TABLE B-4: Determining team roles

factor	description	how roles are assigned
Management	Managers select some or all of the team members	• Managers assign roles • Teams can adjust these roles as necessary
Job, project, or client	The purpose of the team determines roles	• Team tasks dictate the roles people assume • Members perform tasks they have performed before
Training or education	Formal training determines roles	• Members with training or education in a particular area assume roles in that area • For example, someone with an accounting background might handle the budget and financial affairs for the team
Affinity	Members naturally fill unassigned roles if their skills and interests are a good fit for the responsibilities	• Roles are informal • Team leader might ask someone to assume a role to address a team need

More on team roles

When Raymond M. Belbin studied teams and teamwork, he noted that people in teams take on different roles. He divided these into three main types: action-oriented roles, people-oriented roles, and thought-oriented roles. As shown in Figure B-6, people who play action-oriented roles are shapers that challenge the team to improve, implementers that put ideas into action, and finishers, who make sure tasks are completed thoroughly and on time. People-oriented roles include coordinators, who often act as team leaders; team workers, who encourage cooperation; and resource investigators, who explore outside opportunities. The three thought-oriented roles include plants, who present new ideas and approaches; monitor-evaluators, who analyze the options, and specialists, who provide specialized skills.

Source: Belbin Web site, *www.belbin.com*, accessed January 22, 2010.

Establishing Team Rules

During the storming stage, teams should spend time discussing how people work and interact with each other. By openly talking about professional expectations and proper behavior, a team can reduce the number of problems caused by misunderstandings. Team rules should be established by the norming stage. Table B-5 outlines the do's and don'ts of establishing team rules. Figure B-7 lists typical team ground rules. Now that your team is entering the storming stage, you need to establish rules for how the team works together.

ESSENTIAL ELEMENTS

QUICK TIP

Agreeing to basic courtesies makes everyone more conscious of their behavior and improves the work environment.

1. Define basic courtesies

A team can reduce potential problems by having everyone agree to basic rules about courtesy and respect for each other. These can include guidelines such as no character assassination, no blind cover copy (bcc) e-mail messages, and no discussion of personal problems except in private.

2. Outline operating procedures

The professional duties of most team members continue when they join a team. They still need to complete assignments and meet with people in other parts of the business. To manage time and expectations, the team should agree on standards for meeting and working together. For example, establishing a regular place, schedule, and format for group meetings helps develop a routine that makes planning easier.

QUICK TIP

Some teams document their decisions and publish them as a compact or charter.

3. Agree on how to make collective decisions

Groups can make decisions, vote on issues, and solve problems in different ways. Agree to these details as a team. Will you make decisions in formal meetings or as necessary? Does everyone need to participate in collective decisions or can a simple majority of team members decide? How will you resolve problems when no clear consensus emerges?

4. Commit to open communication

Working out communication rules helps to prevent conflict in most groups. The team should commit to open communication that values differing opinions. Some teams have a *no sacred cow* rule, which means any topic can be discussed. Others decide that silence signals agreement with the discussion. However, keep team disagreements, problems, and conflicts private. Do not share them with the larger organization. Communication with people outside of the team should always be positive, professional, and honest.

QUICK TIP

Your team should use any formats the company has already established.

5. Discuss file formats

To share information, team members need to exchange data in the same or similar formats. In an early meeting, agree to common file formats, such as .doc files for text. Discuss where team members should store data and how they can access it. Make sure that everyone on the team has the appropriate software and network access and that everyone can use the materials that each member produces.

YOU TRY IT

1. Use a word processor such as Microsoft Office Word to open the file B-5.doc provided with your Data Files, and save it as Rules.doc in the location where you store your Data Files

2. Read the contents of Rules.doc, which describe a newly formed team

3. Select rules appropriate for the team

4. Save and close Rules.doc, then submit it to your instructor as requested

FIGURE B-7: Ground rules for the Quest Specialty Travel team

Courtesy

- Treat other team members with respect
- Challenge each other constructively
- No personal attacks
- Avoid being defensive
- Help other team members to complete tasks

Communication

- Each person has a chance to speak
- One person talks at a time
- No side discussions, no interruptions
- Be brief and stick to the topic
- When confused, ask
- Allow equal participation of each team member

Operating procedures

- Team meetings are every Tuesday at 9:30 AM in Conference Room B
- All team members are expected to attend meetings on time
- Notify team members if you cannot attend a meeting
- Team leader distributes an agenda
- No electronic interruptions
- End meetings by clarifying who will do what by when

Problems and decisions

- When presenting problems, also present solutions
- Everyone participates in problem solving
- Discuss issues, not people
- Listen and keep an open mind until it is time to decide
- Consensus means we have our say, not get our way

TABLE B-5: Establishing team rules do's and don'ts

guideline	do	don't
Define basic courtesies	Agree to basic rules about courtesy and respect for team members	**Don't** assume team members will observe basic courtesies without establishing ground rules for doing so
Outline operating procedures	• Agree on when the team will meet and how often • Discuss how to make decisions, such as through consensus or voting	**Don't** forget that team members have responsibilities outside of the team
Commit to open communication	• Encourage team members to voice differing opinions • Work out rules about discussing topics, especially those that prevent one team member from dominating • Present a unified front to other members of the organization • Be positive, professional, and honest in your communications with nonteam members	**Don't** share news about team conflicts and disagreements with people outside of the team

Teamwork

Clarifying Team Objectives

When a new group is formed, some team leaders make the mistake of starting to work on project tasks immediately. However, members of the team need to get to know each other before the work begins. They must also develop, understand, and agree on the team objectives. In fact, one way that teams differ from common work groups is how much they define and shape their objectives. Clarifying team objectives helps to create the shared vision and *esprit de corps* (or team spirit) that a team needs to collaborate. After setting ground rules for the Quest Chicago branch office team, you are ready to discuss team objectives.

ESSENTIAL ELEMENTS

1. Clearly define expected outcomes

Management often assigns projects and tasks to a team, but leaves the details to the group itself to work out. Before working on projects, team members should define what they expect to accomplish. They should describe, quantify, and illustrate outcomes in writing. Everyone on the team should feel comfortable with this document before work begins.

> **QUICK TIP**
>
> Starting to work without management's approval can result in lost time and wasted effort.

2. Secure management's approval

Groups can become innovative and develop solutions and action plans that are significantly different from management's original intent. Before starting to work on project tasks, carefully review the team's plan with all interested stakeholders and secure their approval. Often, a manager can highlight opportunities and potential roadblocks that the team has not considered.

3. Decompose the project

Functional decomposition describes breaking down a complex system or set of processes into smaller parts, such as tasks. This means a team should organize a project into small manageable tasks and subtasks. Ideally, a single person or a small group should be able to complete each subtask. The team leader is responsible for any tasks not assigned to other members. Figure B-8 shows the functional decomposition for the publicity tasks in the Quest office-opening project.

4. Clarify each person's role

After team members are assigned to tasks, make sure that everyone knows what they are responsible for. In a team meeting, each member can briefly describe his or her assignment. Other team members can then learn about each person's role. Clarifying roles in a meeting helps the team to see itself as a collection of coordinated people rather than a group of individual workers.

> **QUICK TIP**
>
> Publish the milestones and deadlines where everyone can see them.

5. Set the direction and schedule

Even if a team is not working on a formal project, it can still use basic project management techniques. First, list the tasks the team needs to complete. Also note the major deadlines. Next, the group can discuss which tasks to complete first. Point out **interdependencies** (tasks that need to be completed before another task can begin). Finally, the team should create a timeline or schedule. Identify milestones and critical deadlines. See Figure B-9. As the project continues, update the schedule and provide it to the team. This planning effort creates a roadmap and calendar that keeps everyone on track.

YOU TRY IT

1. Use a word processor such as Microsoft Office Word to open the file B-6.doc provided with your Data Files, and save it as Objectives.doc in the location where you store your Data Files

2. Read the contents of Objectives.doc, which describe a team project

3. Break the project into smaller tasks

4. Save and close Objectives.doc, then submit it to your instructor as requested

FIGURE B-8: Publicity tasks in the Quest office-opening project

Quest Specialty Travel
Chicago office opening: Publicity tasks

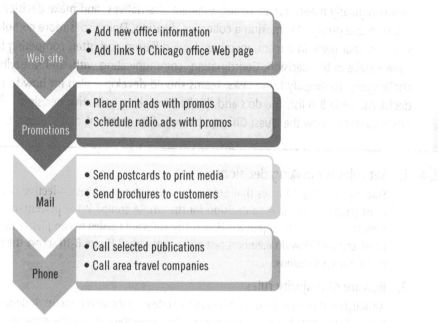

Web site
- Add new office information
- Add links to Chicago office Web page

Promotions
- Place print ads with promos
- Schedule radio ads with promos

Mail
- Send postcards to print media
- Send brochures to customers

Phone
- Call selected publications
- Call area travel companies

FIGURE B-9: Schedule for Quest publicity tasks

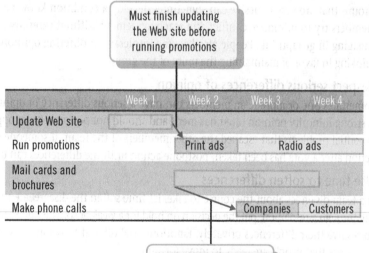

Must finish updating
the Web site before
running promotions

	Week 1	Week 2	Week 3	Week 4
Update Web site				
Run promotions		Print ads	Radio ads	
Mail cards and brochures				
Make phone calls			Companies	Customers

Must start mailing
cards and brochures
before making phone calls

Making Collective Decisions

Teams regularly meet, discuss issues, evaluate alternatives, and make decisions. When a team makes a decision as a group, it is making a collective decision. Doing so is more complicated than making decisions on your own. In a team, members have different and often competing ideas. Each person might have a stake in the decision. Coordinating, communicating with, and satisfying team members can be challenging. To simplify these tasks, teams should develop a plan for how to solve problems and make decisions. Table B-6 lists the do's and don'ts for making collective decisions. Your last planning task is to discuss how the Quest Chicago branch office team will make decisions.

ESSENTIAL ELEMENTS

QUICK TIP

Methods of voting include a show of hands and a secret ballot.

1. Set rules for making decisions

Start by agreeing to rules that govern how the group makes collective decisions. How many people must participate to make a decision for the whole group? What percentage of the group must vote for something for it to be approved? How many votes are needed to completely eliminate an idea from further consideration? How do members cast and count votes? Figure B-10 shows the form Quest Specialty Travel uses for team decisions.

2. Beware of majority rules

Although winning by majority works in most democratic governments, it does not work as well in business teams. A narrow vote such as 51 percent versus 49 percent does not necessarily reflect a clear majority opinion and often creates contention. This is especially true if some team members did not participate in the vote. A narrow vote signals a lack of agreement. You need to spend more time discussing the issue.

QUICK TIP

When a team makes decisions too easily, it can invite an independent expert or assign someone to act as the devil's advocate.

3. Watch out for groupthink

Groups that are very cohesive can sometimes develop a condition known as **groupthink**. When group members try to minimize conflict and reach agreement without carefully analyzing the issues, they are engaging in groupthink. People also become intolerant of differing opinions. They give up independent thinking in favor of maintaining the unity of the group.

4. Respect serious differences of opinion

Sometimes one or more team members can have a serious difference of opinion with the rest of the team. A strong minority opinion often has merit and should not be ignored. An opposing point of view can find potential problems that escaped the other members of the team. If someone still strongly opposes a group action after a vote has been taken, postpone action until the differences can be worked out or reduced.

5. Use time to soften differences

If a team disagrees about the course to take, let time soften the disagreements. Rather than voting or pushing through a resolution, put the decision on hold for a week or so. This allows team members to work together to resolve their differences privately. Emotions cool off and egos soften over time. Revisit the issue when you sense that people are ready to move forward.

YOU TRY IT

1. Use a word processor such as Microsoft Office Word to open the file B-7.doc provided with your Data Files, and save it as Decision.doc in the location where you store your Data Files

2. Read the contents of Decision.doc, which describe a team decision

3. Recommend how the team should handle the decision

4. Save and close Decision.doc, then submit it to your instructor as requested

FIGURE B-10: Quest Specialty Travel form for team decisions

Decisions		
What type of decision does the team need to make?	Who should be involved in this decision?	Who makes the final decision?
○ Financial		○ Team leader
○ Task assignments		○ Team vote
○ Resource assignments		○ Manager
Decision making		
What type of voting will the team use, if any?	How will the team decide?	
○ Majority vote	○ Show of hands	
○ Unanimous vote	○ Written open ballot	
○ Consensus	○ Secret ballot	
○ Ranking options	○ Leader decides	

TABLE B-6: Making collective decisions do's and don'ts

guideline	do	don't
Agree on rules	Set rules for how the team makes decisions	**Don't** start making decisions until you set ground rules
Beware of majority rules	• Be cautious about majority votes • Continue to discuss topics that result in a narrow vote	**Don't** make major decisions based on a narrow majority vote
Watch out for groupthink	• Encourage team members to analyze a decision independently • Respect serious differences of opinion	• **Don't** become intolerant of differing opinions • **Don't** give up independent thinking to conform to the group • **Don't** discount opposing points of view

The power of groupthink

In a recent *Wired* magazine article, Clive Thompson explored the power of the self-fulfilling prophecy, which is closely related to groupthink. He asks, "Do teenagers like Taylor Swift because she's good or because everyone else they know likes her — so hey, she *must* be good, right?" This is an example of groupthink. A group makes a decision based on how it thinks other members of the group will decide.

Thompson describes an experiment conducted by scientists Duncan Watts and Matthew Salganik. "They created a music-downloading Web site," Thompson explains. "They uploaded 48 songs by unknown bands and got people to log in to the site, listen to the songs, then rate and download them. Users could see one another's rankings, and they were influenced in roughly the same way self-fulfilling prophecies are supposed to work. That meant some tunes could become hits—and others duds—partly because of social pressure." After running the experiment many times with different participants, Watts and Salganik concluded that about half of a song's popularity could be attributed to quality and talent.

The rest depended on groupthink. Next, Watts and Salganik decided to find out whether advertising and marketing could influence song choices more than groupthink. Thompson describes the new experiment: "They took the song ratings of one group and inverted them so bottom-ranked music was now at the top. Then they gave these rankings to a fresh set of listeners. In essence, they lied to the new group: They told them that songs that weren't popular with previous listeners actually were." In general, new listeners usually ranked the songs to match the fake ratings. However, some of the truly top-ranked songs began to float up to the top of the list, and the truly low-ranked songs sank to the bottom. More interestingly, people in these groups downloaded fewer songs overall, indicating they sensed the system was rigged. Perhaps these results indicate that introducing doubt or differing opinions can derail groupthink.

Source: Thompson, Clive, "How Group Think Rules What We Like," *Wired,* December 8, 2009.

Technology @ Work: Online Collaboration Tools

Online collaboration tools such as Google Docs and Office Web Apps are forms of software designed to help teams achieve their goals. Online collaboration tools are often organized into three categories: communication tools, conferencing tools, and coordination tools. All of these tools are especially helpful for virtual teams.  Because your team in Chicago is working closely with the Quest Specialty Travel main office in San Diego, Don Novak suggests you review available online collaboration tools.

1. Communication tools

You use electronic communication tools to exchange messages, as in e-mail, or keep in touch with a team and its project, as in a wiki or online group. A **wiki** is a collaborative Web site where team members can share documents and information. For example, Wikipedia (*en.wikipedia.org*), an online encyclopedia, is a well-known wiki. An online group such as a Windows Live (*home.live.com*) group works in a similar way. See Figure B-11.

2. Conferencing tools

You use online conferencing tools to quickly share information. For example, instant messaging is a form of basic online conferencing. Videoconferencing, in which team members can see and hear each other on networked computers, is more sophisticated. Similar to videoconferencing, you use Web conferencing to conduct online meetings, especially when you want to share one user's desktop.

More recent conferencing tools include those that let you and at least one other team member access a shared application or document from your computers at the same time. For example, Office Web Apps, available with Microsoft Office provide online versions of some Office software and let you store, edit, and share documents with other Office Web Apps users. See Figure B-12.

> **QUICK TIP**
>
> You can also use online event tools such as Meetup (*www.meetup.com*) to organize physical meetings.

3. Coordination tools

This category of online collaboration tools includes online calendars, such as Google Calendar (*www.google.com/calendar*), which lets you or your team schedule events and notify team members. Project management systems such as Zoho Projects (*projects.zoho.com/home.na*) help you schedule, track, and chart the steps in a project as it is being completed. Blogs and social network software such as LinkedIn (*www.linkedin.com*) also fall into this category.

1. Open a Web browser such as Microsoft Internet Explorer or Mozilla Firefox, and go to the Web sites for two of the online collaboration tools mentioned in this unit

2. Log on or create a free account at each Web site, and then find a description of the tool

3. Press the Print Screen key to take a screen shot of each Web page, open a word-processing program such as Microsoft Word, press Ctrl+V to paste each screen shot in a new document, then send the document to your instructor

FIGURE B-11: Setting up a Windows Live group

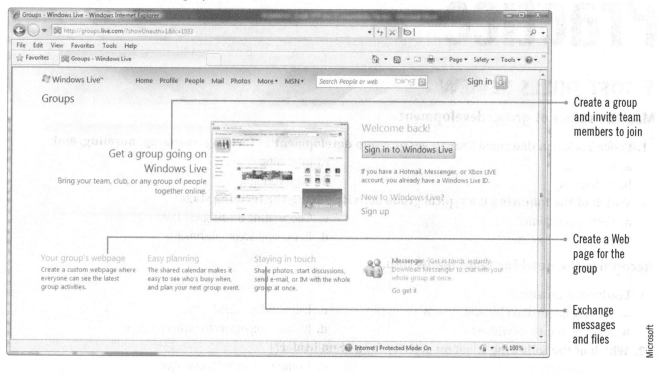

- Create a group and invite team members to join
- Create a Web page for the group
- Exchange messages and files

Microsoft

FIGURE B-12: Office Web Apps

- Document stored on Windows Live
- Microsoft Word document being edited in Office Web Apps

Microsoft

Teamwork

Microsoft

Practice

▼ SOFT SKILLS REVIEW

Map the stages of group development.

1. Bruce Tuckman described four stages of group development as forming, storming, norming, and:
   - **a.** reforming
   - **b.** performing
   - **c.** informing
   - **d.** habit forming

2. Which of the following is a typical group activity during the forming stage?
   - **a.** Getting acquainted
   - **b.** Discussing objectives
   - **c.** Cooperating on assigned tasks
   - **d.** Reviewing accomplishments

Recognize the need for team leadership.

1. Leadership means:
   - **a.** relaying information between groups
   - **b.** reaching consensus without conflict
   - **c.** being independent
   - **d.** influencing others to achieve a goal

2. Which of the following is *not* an activity for a team leader?
   - **a.** Manage conflict
   - **b.** Participate in team assignments
   - **c.** Communicate with management
   - **d.** Report slow team members to management

Select team members.

1. Many managers say that the most important characteristic to consider when making team selections is:
   - **a.** attitude
   - **b.** skills
   - **c.** experience
   - **d.** friendship

2. What should you do before selecting members for a team?
   - **a.** List employees who are loyal to the company
   - **b.** Establish team rules
   - **c.** Complete the *norming* stage
   - **d.** List specialized skills you need

Choose the optimal team size.

1. What have researchers found in general about team size?
   - **a.** Small groups are better than large groups
   - **b.** Large groups are better than small groups
   - **c.** Groups should have exactly six members
   - **d.** Groups should never have only three members

2. What does a deliberative group do?
   - **a.** Complete projects that demand quick solutions
   - **b.** Meet online because they are not in the same physical location
   - **c.** Discuss or debate a topic
   - **d.** Focus on tasks

Define common team roles.

1. Which of the following is *not* a type of team member in the *doing* role?
   - **a.** Implementer
   - **b.** Shaper
   - **c.** Specialist
   - **d.** Finisher

2. Which of the following is a factor in assigning a role to a team member?
   - **a.** Influence
   - **b.** Training or education
   - **c.** Affection
   - **d.** Effort

Establish team rules.

1. During what stage should teams establish rules?

   a. Storming

   b. Norming

   c. Adjourning

   d. Forming

2. Which of the following is *not* an example of a typical team rule?

   a. One person talks at a time

   b. When presenting problems, also present solutions

   c. Treat other team members with respect

   d. Consensus means we get our way

Clarify team objectives.

1. One way that teams differ from common work groups is:

   a. how long they meet

   b. how much teams define and shape their objectives

   c. how many objectives they have

   d. how often teams meet objectives

2. Which of the following is a project management technique that teams should use?

   a. Point out interdependencies

   b. List tasks the team must complete

   c. Rank tasks the team must complete

   d. All of the above

Make collective decisions.

1. What is a collective decision?

   a. Making a decision as a group

   b. Making a decision as an individual

   c. Collecting votes on a decision

   d. A majority decision

2. When group members try to minimize conflict and reach agreement without carefully analyzing the issues, they are engaging in:

   a. groupthink

   b. groupdecision

   c. teamthink

   d. conflict management

Technology @ Work: Online collaboration tools

1. Which of the following is *not* a category of online collaboration tool?

   a. Communication tools

   b. Conferencing tools

   c. Conforming tools

   d. Coordination tools

2. An example of an online communication tool where team members can share documents and information is:

   a. Windows Live groups

   b. Zoho Projects

   c. LinkedIn

   d. Meetup

▼ CRITICAL THINKING QUESTIONS

1. Why do you think teams and other groups experience groupthink? What can a group do to avoid groupthink?

2. Which type of role do you usually play in a group or team? Describe the activities you perform in this role.

3. Recall a time when you were a member of a small team. Then recall when you were a member of a large team. Which did you prefer and why?

4. Have you ever been a team leader? Compare being a team leader to being a member of the team.

5. Think about an ineffective team you participated in or observed. What prevented that team from being effective?

▼ INDEPENDENT CHALLENGE 1

You are an administrative assistant at Newberry Heating & Cooling, a contracting company in Columbus, Ohio. Your supervisor, Joanne Burton, is organizing a team for the Customer Service department. She wants to break down each task employees perform when handling customer complaints. She has started to create a diagram in a Microsoft PowerPoint presentation that lists the types of activities employees should perform. See Figure B-13. She gives you a description from the employee handbook on handling customer complaints, and asks you to complete the diagram.

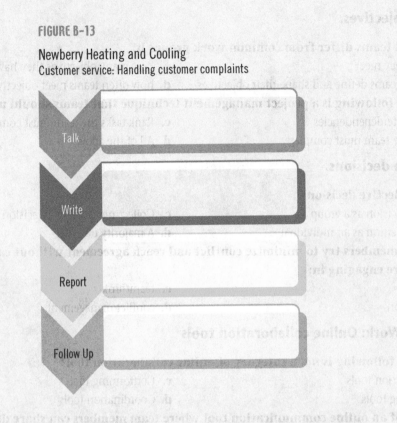

FIGURE B-13

Newberry Heating and Cooling
Customer service: Handling customer complaints

Talk

Write

Report

Follow Up

a. Use word-processing software such as Microsoft Office Word to open the file **B-8.doc** provided with your Data Files, and save it as **Tasks.doc** in the location where you store your Data Files.
b. Use presentation software such as Microsoft Office PowerPoint to open the file **B-9.ppt** provided with your Data Files, and save it as **Task List.ppt** in the location where you store your Data Files.
c. Complete the diagram in Task List.ppt based on the description in Tasks.doc.
d. Submit the files to your instructor as requested.

▼ INDEPENDENT CHALLENGE 2

PT at Home is a business in Syracuse, New York, that provides physical therapy services to people in their homes. George Lambert, the owner of the company, has an idea for a new piece of exercise equipment that he wants to use to improve people's back strength. He is also organizing a team to design, test, and build the equipment. George asks you to help him create a schedule for the team. See Figure B-14.

FIGURE B-14

	Week 1	Week 2	Week 3	Week 4
Design sample equipment	▮			
Test equipment				
Build equipment				
Retest equipment				

a. Use word-processing software such as Microsoft Office Word to open the file **B-10.doc** provided with your Data Files, and save it as **Milestones.doc** in the location where you store your Data Files.

b. Read the description of the PT at Home schedule in Milestones.doc. Based on those descriptions, complete the schedule shown at the beginning of Milestones.doc. Be sure to indicate interdependencies.

c. Submit the document and presentation to your instructor as requested.

▼ REAL LIFE INDEPENDENT CHALLENGE

Whether you are a member of a group or team at work or not, you can continue to develop your group skills online. You can join an online group for free at one of the following Web sites:

- Campfire: *campfirenow.com*
- Facebook Groups: *www.facebook.com*
- Google Groups: *groups.google.com*
- Ning: *www.ning.com*
- Yahoo! Groups: *groups.yahoo.com*
- Zoho Wiki: *wiki.zoho.com*

a. Visit at least three of the group Web sites listed in this exercise.

b. Find a Web site that lets you join a group without being invited. Then look for groups that relate to your career interests. Learn what types of information and services the group offers.

c. Find a Web site where you must create your own group. Start a group and invite friends and classmates who share your career interests to join.

▼ TEAM CHALLENGE

You are working for Peachtree Landscapers, a landscaping company in Atlanta, Georgia. Liz Montoya, the owner of Peachtree Landscapes, is organizing employees into teams. She suggests that you meet physically or online as a team and then create a team contract.

a. Working independently, research *team contracts* online or at a library.

b. Working with your group, write a sentence that describes the purpose of a team contract.

c. Next, list the types of information a team contract should include. For example, most team contracts include a section that lists the team's goals.

d. Complete the outline of the team contract as a team, and then submit it to your instructor as requested.

▼ BE THE CRITIC

You are working for a training center that trains people to qualify for a variety of jobs in manufacturing and technology. Marilyn Cosgrove, the director of the center, wants to organize the center's employees into teams. She has created the list of team rules shown in Figure B-15 that teams can use as a starting point. Analyze these rules, and then list which ones are strong and which are weak. Send the list to your instructor as requested.

FIGURE B-15

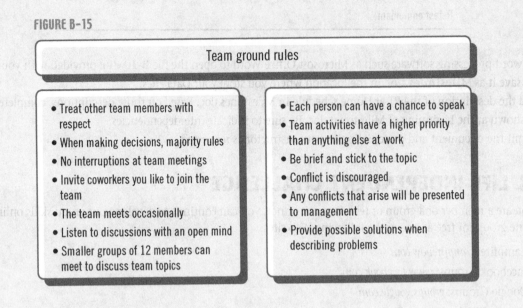

Team ground rules

- Treat other team members with respect
- When making decisions, majority rules
- No interruptions at team meetings
- Invite coworkers you like to join the team
- The team meets occasionally
- Listen to discussions with an open mind
- Smaller groups of 12 members can meet to discuss team topics

- Each person can have a chance to speak
- Team activities have a higher priority than anything else at work
- Be brief and stick to the topic
- Conflict is discouraged
- Any conflicts that arise will be presented to management
- Provide possible solutions when describing problems

Building and Developing Teams

When discussing teams, most businesses focus on who should be included on the team, what the team should be responsible for, and who should lead the team. Another critical but sometimes overlooked decision is how to develop the group so that it works together cohesively and successfully. In this unit, you will learn about how teams develop and what you can do to help guide a group toward meeting its goals.  You are working as an assistant office manager to Don Novak at the Quest Specialty Travel branch office in Chicago, Illinois. After one team successfully organized the grand opening of the Chicago office, Don asks you and other staff members to form another team to create a training guide for new employees.

OBJECTIVES

Understand the benefits of working in teams

Foster relationships

Overcome resistance

Use team-building activities

Create a team identity

Cope with conflict and ego

Deal with difficult team members

Celebrate successes

Understanding the Benefits of Working in Teams

Because people are naturally social, they need to interact with others regularly. Working as part of a team can meet this need. Depending on the group dynamics, a team can offer additional benefits or drawbacks to its members. **Group dynamics** are the ways that people interact with each other. This includes how they develop roles, establish relationships, and influence each other. See Figure C-1. If a team has poor group dynamics, members are often in conflict. They avoid group activities and work independently, which makes the team less productive. When a team has good group dynamics, members get along with each other and are motivated to contribute to the team and its goals. This type of team is considered a well-developed group and produces high-quality work. It also provides benefits to each member and to the group as a whole. See Figure C-2. Now that Don has established the training guide team, he suggests you learn about the benefits of working in teams.

DETAILS

Well-developed teams offer its members the following benefits:

- **Satisfy a sense of belonging**

  In general, people need to feel they are a welcome and valued part of their environment. They seek a sense of belonging in their social and professional lives. Both formal and informal groups help to satisfy needs for friendship and support. As you work with a team, consider ways to welcome members and help them feel they belong.

- **Enhance feelings of identity and self-esteem**

  At work, people often evaluate their role within the larger organization. They want to know that they are adding value to the business. Being a part of a team working on important tasks can reinforce members' feelings of worth, identity, and self-esteem.

- **Balance workloads and reduce stress**

  When a single person is responsible for a significant project, he or she can quickly become overwhelmed by the amount of work that needs to be done. Assigning the project to a team distributes the same amount of work to more people. Each person should be responsible for roughly the same amount of work. Balancing the workload creates a shared sense of responsibility and can reduce the stress on each team member.

- **Meet needs for social exchange and interaction**

  People don't interact on a purely professional level all of the time. Even in an office, they need to communicate with others socially. Talking about topics outside of work and sharing parts of their personal life strengthens bonds between people, especially when they are members of the same team.

- **Create a support network**

  Departments and workers often have competing interests and objectives. Frequently, this competition leads to conflict. If the conflict involves two teams, it seems less personal than a conflict involving two people. If a single team member has a confrontation with another person in the business, the team can offer support and suggestions for resolving the conflict.

FIGURE C-1: Group dynamics

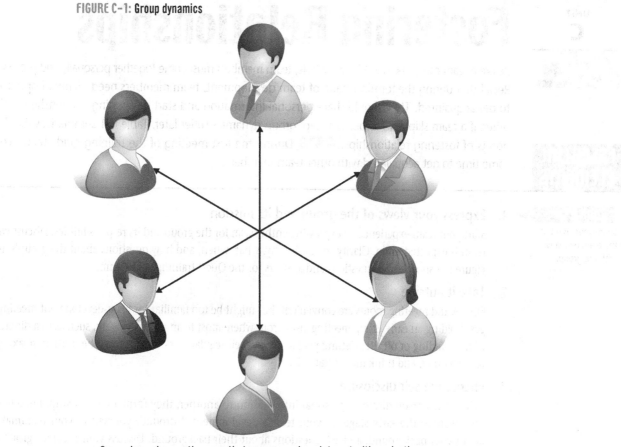

Group dynamics are the ways that group members interact with each other

FIGURE C-2: Benefits of a well-developed group

To each member		To the group as a whole
Personal	Professional	Team
• Satisfaction • Self-confidence • Self-esteem	• Achievement • Balanced workload	• Support network • Commitment • Achievement

Fostering Relationships

Before a team can work as a cohesive whole, team members must come together personally and professionally. Recall that during the forming stage of team development, team members need plenty of opportunities to get acquainted. They should share personal information and start developing relationships with each other. If a team skips this important step, group dynamics suffer later. Table C-1 summarizes the do's and don'ts of fostering relationships. During the first meeting of the training guide team, you take some time to get acquainted with other team members.

ESSENTIAL ELEMENTS

1. Express your views of the group and its mission

Start your team experience by expressing enthusiasm for the group and its responsibilities. Discuss what the team is expected to do. Clarify the basic why, what, when, and how questions about the group's mission. Figure C-3 shows these questions and answers for the Quest training guide team.

2. Take it outside

Offices and meeting rooms are convenient, but might be too familiar for team-development meetings. Suggest holding an early group meeting away from where most team members work, such as in a different part of the building or off site. Getting people out of their regular work environment helps them relax, open up to each other, and think more creatively.

3. Encourage self-disclosure

When one person discloses personal information to another, they form a relationship. Encourage self-disclosure in the early stages of your team's development. Introduce yourself to your teammates, talk about your background, and ask questions about their background. Discuss your previous group experiences and share your goals with the other members. Self-disclosure quickly changes a simple group into a cohesive team.

4. Build in open communication

A common mistake that team leaders and supervisors make is to talk too much during the first team meetings. A team needs lots of open conversations as it starts to form. If you are a team leader, set up meetings and activities so they encourage people to interact. Assign people to lead parts of the discussion or report on agenda items. Keep the atmosphere informal and relaxed to encourage participation. You can keep track of the communication by completing a chart similar to the one shown in Figure C-4. Tally each time a team member speaks to someone else or to the group as a whole.

5. Distribute power and responsibility among the members

People are more likely to embrace the team and become active members if they have a stake in it. One of the best ways to accomplish this is to be involved. Accept responsibility for at least one major task. If you are the team leader, distribute power by delegating at least one task to each member. For large tasks or decisions, form smaller groups that set their own direction. Ask everyone to report on their progress at team meetings so they are accountable to the team.

YOU TRY IT

1. Use a word processor such as Microsoft Office Word to open the file C-1.doc provided with your Data Files, and save it as Relationships.doc in the location where you store your Data Files

2. Read the contents of Relationships.doc, which describe group interactions

3. Identify ways the group can foster relationships

4. Save and close Relationships.doc, then submit it to your instructor as requested

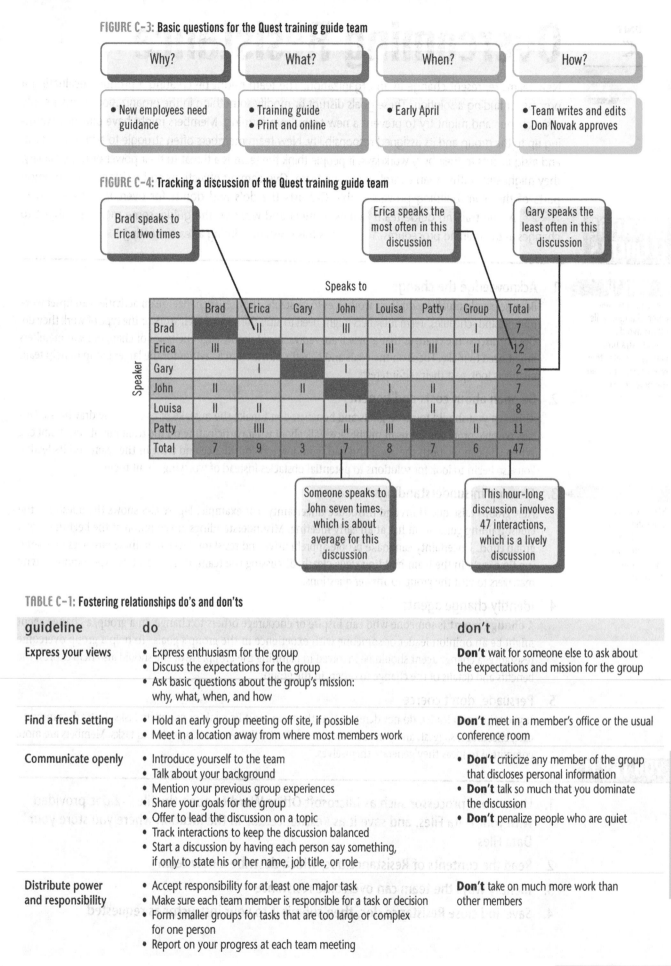

FIGURE C-3: Basic questions for the Quest training guide team

Why?	What?	When?	How?
• New employees need guidance	• Training guide • Print and online	• Early April	• Team writes and edits • Don Novak approves

FIGURE C-4: Tracking a discussion of the Quest training guide team

Brad speaks to Erica two times

Erica speaks the most often in this discussion

Gary speaks the least often in this discussion

Speaks to

Speaker	Brad	Erica	Gary	John	Louisa	Patty	Group	Total
Brad		II		III	I		I	7
Erica	III		I	III	III	II		12
Gary		I		I				2
John	II		II		I	II		7
Louisa	II	II		I		II	I	8
Patty		IIII		II	III		II	11
Total	7	9	3	7	8	7	6	47

Someone speaks to John seven times, which is about average for this discussion

This hour-long discussion involves 47 interactions, which is a lively discussion

TABLE C-1: Fostering relationships do's and don'ts

guideline	do	don't
Express your views	• Express enthusiasm for the group • Discuss the expectations for the group • Ask basic questions about the group's mission: why, what, when, and how	**Don't** wait for someone else to ask about the expectations and mission for the group
Find a fresh setting	• Hold an early group meeting off site, if possible • Meet in a location away from where most members work	**Don't** meet in a member's office or the usual conference room
Communicate openly	• Introduce yourself to the team • Talk about your background • Mention your previous group experiences • Share your goals for the group • Offer to lead the discussion on a topic • Track interactions to keep the discussion balanced • Start a discussion by having each person say something, if only to state his or her name, job title, or role	• **Don't** criticize any member of the group that discloses personal information • **Don't** talk so much that you dominate the discussion • **Don't** penalize people who are quiet
Distribute power and responsibility	• Accept responsibility for at least one major task • Make sure each team member is responsible for a task or decision • Form smaller groups for tasks that are too large or complex for one person • Report on your progress at each team meeting	**Don't** take on much more work than other members

Teamwork

Overcoming Resistance

New teams represent change in an organization. The team might be creating a product, evaluating a process, or finding a solution. These goals disrupt or modify something in the organization. Some people resist change and might try to prevent a new team from forming. Members might have difficulty warming up to the group and its assigned responsibility. New team members often struggle to add shared tasks and assignments to their busy workdays. If people think the team is a threat to their power or responsibility, they might stifle rather than contribute to the team. Overcoming objections and resistance are common parts of the team-building process. Table C-2 lists the do's and don'ts for overcoming resistance.

ESSENTIAL ELEMENTS

 As the training guide team begins to meet and work on the guide, some members object to changes in the training procedures. You discuss this resistance during a team meeting.

QUICK TIP
Some people welcome change, while others avoid it. Spend extra time with teammates that seem hesitant to join the new group.

1. Acknowledge the changes
Because people usually want their work lives to be stable, they resist change. Team activities can upset work routines and schedules. Team members might need to alter the pace of their work or the type of work they do. Openly discuss the changes that a new team represents. Acknowledge the types of changes team members might need to make. Focus on the goals and benefits of the team activities for the larger group to help team members look past their self-interests.

2. Be open about costs and benefits
Although you should focus on goals and benefits, don't make the mistake of overlooking drawbacks. Discuss possible problems the team might face. Talk about what participating on the team might cost members. When you can see both the good and bad, you develop confidence and trust in the team and its leader. You also begin to look for solutions to potential obstacles instead of worrying about them.

QUICK TIP
Some teams reserve a question-and-answer time in all group meetings to address misunderstandings.

3. Clear up misunderstandings
New groups raise questions and introduce uncertainty. For example, Figure C-5 shows the questions the Quest training guide team has at an early meeting. Misunderstandings are common at the beginning of a group effort. Uncertainty can make people apprehensive and resistant. Overcome these obstacles by spending time early in the team-building stage clearly discussing the team, its role, and its expectations. Invite managers to visit the group to answer questions.

4. Identify change agents
A **change agent** is someone who can inspire or encourage others to change. In a group, a change agent might be an opinion leader or someone with experience in the group's goals. To help a group overcome resistance, a change agent should be involved in planning the group. He or she should also help express the benefits and details of the change to others in the group.

5. Persuade, don't coerce
If you are a team leader, do not demand that the team meet its goals or complete tasks. Instead, communicate, encourage, suggest, and persuade people. Ideally, let the team set its goals and tasks. Members are more committed to ideas they generate themselves.

YOU TRY IT

1. Use a word processor such as Microsoft Office Word to open the file C-2.doc provided with your Data Files, and save it as Resistance.doc in the location where you store your Data Files

2. Read the contents of Resistance.doc, which describe a new team

3. Identify ways the team can overcome resistance

4. Save and close Resistance.doc, then submit it to your instructor as requested

FIGURE C-5: Questions raised about training guide team efforts

TABLE C-2: Overcoming resistance do's and don'ts

guideline	do	don't
Acknowledge the changes	• Understand why people resist change • Discuss changes that a new team introduces • Talk about the types of changes team members need to make • Identify benefits of team activities	**Don't** downplay the effect of changes; be realistic
Discuss costs and benefits	• Talk about problems the team might face • Identify what participating on the team might cost members • Discuss the pros and the cons	**Don't** overlook the drawbacks of team activities or being a team member
Clear up misunderstandings	• In the first few meetings, discuss the purpose of the team and what it is expected to accomplish • Invite managers to answer team questions	• **Don't** discourage questions • **Don't** let misunderstandings linger
Be a team leader	• Identify a change agent in the group • Work closely with the change agent, or serve as the change agent in the group • Persuade and encourage your teammates	**Don't** demand that teammates complete tasks or meet goals

Teamwork

Using Team-Building Activities

Team building involves activities designed to improve a team's performance. Activities include bonding exercises, group games, simulations, and retreats. Some companies send their high-profile teams to **challenge courses** or **ropes courses**. These are elaborate outdoor activities patterned after military obstacle courses. They require the entire team's cooperation to help each participant overcome barriers. Although most new teams do not have the luxury of a professional retreat or challenge course, they can still use team-building activities to get acquainted and learn to trust each other. To make the training guide team more cohesive, you and your teammates consider using some team-building activities.

ESSENTIAL ELEMENTS

1. Invest in your first meeting

First impressions count, especially when a new team is figuring out what the group is all about. Plan the details of your first team meeting to make it a positive experience. Choose a comfortable and convenient location. Identify a time when people will be alert and attentive. Set the agenda and prepare handouts and other supporting materials in advance. Consider having refreshments available to make people more comfortable and relaxed.

> **QUICK TIP**
> To conduct icebreaker activities, try using a facilitator, someone who is good at organizing and conducting group events.

2. Use icebreaker activities

Icebreakers are exercises that help a group begin to form itself into a team. Generally, icebreakers encourage participants to get to know each other. Most icebreaking activities are games that involve sharing personal history and information. Table C-3 summarizes a few popular icebreakers you can use with almost any team.

3. Create a warm-up task

Instead of working on team tasks at the first meeting, start with one or more warm-up tasks. These tasks are not games or exercises, but rather a brief, low-cost activity related to the team's purpose. Figure C-6 shows a few examples. After a team learns to work together on small activities, it can apply these skills to more complicated tasks.

> **QUICK TIP**
> Setting ground rules helps the team learn to work together and establishes policies that define acceptable behavior.

4. Develop the ground rules

Establishing the procedures and protocols the group will use is an excellent team-building activity. People typically are motivated to shape policies that affect them personally. Discuss ground rules for general behavior, communication, meetings, voting, and decision making.

5. Provide training if necessary

Some teams take on projects that require special skills or know-how. They might need special training or invite a specialist to the group. Workshops, seminars, and instructor-led classes improve the knowledge and skill of team members. Training also lets team members work together and get to know each other.

YOU TRY IT

1. Use a word processor such as Microsoft Office Word to open the file C-3.doc provided with your Data Files, and save it as Team Building.doc in the location where you store your Data Files

2. Read the contents of Team Building.doc, which describe a new group

3. Identify how the group can develop into a team

4. Save and close Team Building.doc, then submit it to your instructor as requested

FIGURE C-6: Examples of warm-up tasks

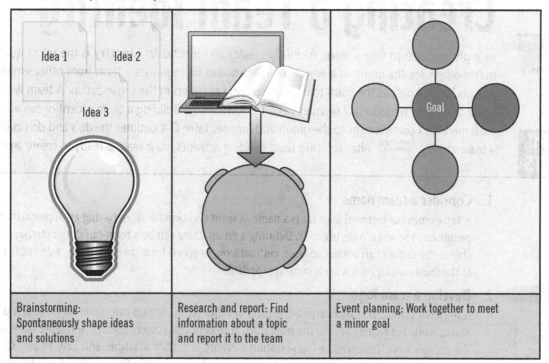

| Brainstorming: Spontaneously shape ideas and solutions | Research and report: Find information about a topic and report it to the team | Event planning: Work together to meet a minor goal |

TABLE C-3: Sample icebreakers

name	description	goal
Little Known Fact	• Introduce yourself to someone in the group you don't know well • Give your name, department or role, and length of service • Offer one little known fact about yourself	To provide memorable details that a teammate can use in future interactions
Personal Interview	• Find a partner you don't already know • Spend five minutes interviewing your partner • Spend five minutes being interviewed by your partner • Introduce your partner to the entire team	To spark personal relationships among team members
Two Truths and a Lie	• Introduce yourself to the team • Make three personal statements such as "My favorite food is" • Two of the personal statements should be true and one is untrue • Invite the team to vote on which statement is the lie	To encourage self-disclosure

Creating a Team Identity

As a group develops into a team, it usually creates an identity. An **identity** is the set of qualities that makes others see the group as a whole. An identity also distinguishes a team from other similar groups. A team identity defines the team to its members and to others in the organization. A team with a strong sense of identity tends to feel unique, valued, and cohesive. Building a team's identity can also increase each member's commitment to the group and morale. Table C-4 outlines the do's and don'ts of creating a team identity. After enjoying team-building activities, your team is ready to create an identity.

ESSENTIAL ELEMENTS

1. Consider a team name

A key element of personal identity is a name. A team also benefits from having an appropriate name that people can use when referring to it. Defining a group name can be a team-building exercise. Some teams choose the name of an animal, mascot, cultural icon, or sports team. In other cases, a descriptive title such as the *Quest training guide team* is more appropriate.

2. Develop a team logo

A **logo** is a graphic that represents a company or other group. A team can create a logo to brand the group and its work. See Figure C-7. Use the team logo on reports, coversheets, memos, and other material to brand the group's work. Inexpensive logo-creation software is readily available and easy to use. Groups on a budget can select a shape or icon from a stock clip-art collection (such as the one included in Microsoft Office). Groups can develop several logos and then vote on the one they want to use.

3. Explore slogans, songs, and cheers

Some teams develop a team slogan, song, or even a cheer. The latter are popular in some cultures and a source of pride for team members. Chants, cheers, and slogans are often useful when a team is competing against another group, such as a department or shift.

4. Develop visual reminders

Teams create an identity to remind members that they belong to the team. Visual reminders are images that reinforce a message or idea. Some teams create vinyl banners, posters, or signs with the group name and logo and display them in shared work areas. These visual reminders offer visibility for the team.

5. Invest in branded apparel and gifts

As a source of incentives, branded items are a popular option. Teams can embroider their name and logo on shirts and jackets, for example. They can also purchase branded coffee mugs, notebooks, and other desk accessories. Team-branded items can be used as inexpensive rewards that also heighten the sense of group identity when team members wear or use them.

YOU TRY IT

1. Use a word processor such as Microsoft Office Word to open the file C-4.doc provided with your Data Files, and save it as Identity.doc in the location where you store your Data Files

2. Read the contents of Identity.doc, which describe a new group

3. Identify ways the group can create a team identity

4. Save and close Identity.doc, then submit it to your instructor as requested

FIGURE C-7: Group logos

| Quest Specialty Travel company logo | Quest Chicago branch office team logo | Quest training guide team logo |

TABLE C-4: Creating a team identity do's and don'ts

guideline	do	don't
Name your team	Select an appropriate and easy-to-remember name in a team meeting	**Don't** choose a name that might offend anyone in or outside of the company
Use images to build an identity	• Create a team logo • Use the logo on anything the team produces • Print the team slogan on a poster or banner • Post signs with the team name and logo where the team works • Add the team name and logo to items that can be used as incentive gifts	• **Don't** select a logo without involving all of the team members • **Don't** force your team identity where others might resent it

Using social networks for team building

Companies large and small are using social networks to market their products and connect with customers. Some are also using the same Web tools to create internal networks for teams. Younger workers in particular are comfortable with the tools provided by a social network. Teams in general can quickly establish an identity and simplify communication. Companies are finding that social networks are an efficient way for teams to get to know one another, share information, and recruit others to the team. However, as Heather Green writes in a recent *BusinessWeek* article, "Setting up a corporate version of a social network has its own challenges, as well. Companies have to build in safeguards to ensure that they can track the discussions and document sharing, to be certain that employees comply with government regulations and don't tumble into legal hot water." One of the main benefits of using an internal

social network is decreasing e-mail traffic. Social networks make collaboration easy. Green relates the case of the Film Foundation in Los Angeles, which is using a team to manage an educational film program. "Workers can archive research documents, share calendars, chat, and blog. A team of 60 researchers, writers, teachers, and filmmakers is putting together a curriculum, distributed free to schools across the country that teaches students how to understand the visual language of films. By having members brainstorm, review each other's work, and prepare budgets on the network, the Film Foundation believes it can cut by half the amount of time it takes to create the materials."

Source: Green, Heather, "In-House Social Networks," *BusinessWeek*, September 23, 2007.

Teamwork

Coping with Conflict and Ego

Recall that during the storming stage of team development, members come into conflict with other people in the group. Figure C-8 shows the concerns of most groups in the storming stage. Conflict often results when a team member's ego becomes overcharged. The term **ego** is a part of Sigmund Freud's model of the human psyche and refers to a person's self-esteem. The ego is partly responsible for peoples' drive and ambition and causes them to seek status and authority. A team member is being egotistical when he or she claims credit for the work of others or dominates discussions or meetings. Egotistical team members also openly remind others of their superiority or excellence and exert power they don't have. Table C-5 lists the do's and don'ts for coping with conflict and ego. Now that your team has established its purpose and identity, some members are coming into conflict with other members. You want to understand how to cope with emotion and ego during this stage of team development.

QUICK TIP

When people are comfortable with their ego, they feel more confident and willing to have new experiences.

1. Remember that everyone has an ego

Although the term *egotistical* often describes behavior to avoid, having an ego is a natural part of being human. Egos help people define themselves. They reflect feelings of self-worth, confidence, and importance. When protecting their egos, people can be defensive and even destructive. Avoid bruising the egos of others, and try to boost people's self-esteem whenever you can.

2. Acknowledge your superstars

People with a track record of accomplishment sometimes have an inflated ego that goes along with their success. Be aware that team superstars need recognition. You might need to tolerate some egotistical behavior from key people so they do not withdraw their contributions.

QUICK TIP

Focusing on the greater good contrasts with an egotistical approach, which focuses on the needs of a single individual.

3. Focus on the greater good

When someone's ego does get out of hand, it can cause conflicts in the group. To avoid this, discuss points of contention from the perspective of the team, company, or clients. Emphasize that everyone is working together for the greater good. When you openly focus on the needs of the team or the organization, it is harder for someone to behave egotistically.

4. Be direct

If someone's ego causes him or her to behave aggressively, dominate meetings, or take credit for the team's efforts, the team leader should respond directly. Team members can also respond directly to maintain the team's cohesiveness. Calmly state your positions, object to actions or opinions you disagree with, and make reasoned counter arguments.

QUICK TIP

Be careful that you do this without sounding patronizing.

5. Call them by name

When someone is behaving arrogantly, it can be disarming to address him or her by name. Use their name frequently as you speak. Calling someone by name can help you take control of the dialogue and command their attention.

1. Use a word processor such as Microsoft Office Word to open the file C-5.doc provided with your Data Files, and save it as Ego.doc in the location where you store your Data Files

2. Read the contents of Ego.doc, which describe a group in conflict

3. Identify how a team member's ego is affecting the team

4. Save and close Ego.doc, then submit it to your instructor as requested

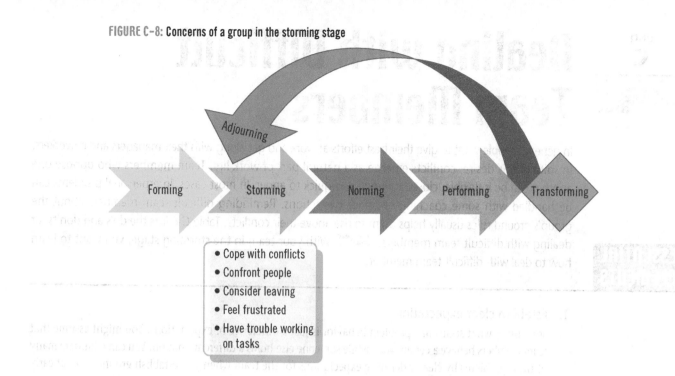

FIGURE C-8: Concerns of a group in the storming stage

Forming → Storming → Norming → Performing → Transforming

Adjourning

- Cope with conflicts
- Confront people
- Consider leaving
- Feel frustrated
- Have trouble working on tasks

TABLE C-5: Coping with conflict and ego do's and don'ts

guideline	do	don't
Recognize team members' egos	• Keep in mind that everyone has an ego • Remember that people are often defensive or even destructive when protecting their ego • Boost the self-esteem of your teammates • Acknowledge the team's superstars	• **Don't** bruise the egos of your teammates • **Don't** alienate your superstars, or they might withdraw their contributions
Resolve conflicts	• Emphasize that everyone is working together for the greater good • Soften conflict by discussing what is best for the company or team • Respond directly and immediately to aggressive behavior • Stay calm and objective • When talking to an egotistical person, repeat their name frequently	• **Don't** let one team member's ego overtake the mission of the team • **Don't** force your team identity where others might resent it • **Don't** wait to respond to destructive behavior by an egotistical team member

Understanding the storming stage

In an article for the Human Resources department at the Massachusetts Institute of Technology, Judith Stein describes the storming stage in team development. She organizes the stage into three areas: feelings, behaviors, and tasks.

Feelings: After the team gets acquainted and starts to work, members "discover that the team can't live up to all of their early excitement and expectations." Some members feel frustrated and want the team to progress more quickly. Other members are worried that the team won't meet its goals. Stein explains that "During the storming stage, members are trying to see how the team will respond to differences and how it will handle conflict."

Behaviors: Team members are not as polite with each other as they were in the norming stage. They begin to disagree about the team's goals, expectations, roles, and responsibilities. They also become frustrated with each other and with the team leader.

Tasks: Stein says that during the storming stage, a team needs "to refocus on its goals, perhaps breaking larger goals down into smaller, achievable steps." Learning how to cooperate with others to do this and to manage conflict gradually leads the team out of the storming stage.

Source: Stein, Judith, "Using the Stages of Team Development," Human Resources at MIT Web page, *http://web.mit.edu/hr/oed/learn/teams/art_stages.html*, accessed January 19, 2010.

Teamwork

Dealing with Difficult Team Members

In general, people want to give their best efforts at work and get along with their managers and coworkers. In spite of this desire, conflicts emerge as a natural part of work life. Team members who oppose one another can be inflexible, closed-minded, and quick to anger. In most cases, interpersonal problems can be handled with some coaching or minor corrections. Reminding difficult team members about the group's ground rules usually helps them to rise above their conflicts. Table C-6 lists the do's and don'ts for dealing with difficult team members. With your team in the storming stage, you want to learn how to deal with difficult team members.

1. Establish clear expectations

Sometimes what seems like problem behavior is just a difference of expectations. You might assume that team members behave a certain way, while someone else holds a different opinion. You can eliminate many of these problems by clearly defining expectations for the team when you establish ground rules at early meetings.

2. Do your homework

Problems that appear in a group often have their roots in other places. The impolite exchange between two people at a meeting might only be the latest in a history of conflicts. Instead of responding to conflict by treating the symptoms, learn more about the conflict. Who or what is causing the problem? What are the opposing points of view? Who else is involved?

3. Resolve leadership uncertainties

People often clash when they don't sense any clear leadership. They are in conflict because they are competing to control the team. If neither person is supposed to be in charge, the team leader should step in and make it clear who is leading the group.

4. Deal directly with problems

When a conflict threatens a team's cohesiveness and focus, the team leader and other team members need to respond to the problem directly. Otherwise, the problem is likely to escalate. See Figure C-9. Identify inappropriate behaviors, but do not attack a person. Discuss what is unacceptable, and ask the offending persons how they recommend resolving the conflict. If a person is not a good fit for the team, the team leader should remove them from the team.

QUICK TIP

Exhaust your other options before making drastic cuts or changes. Consult with the human resources office about removing someone from a team.

5. Call in reinforcements

Sometimes behavior may get out of hand or a difficult employee is unresponsive to your best efforts at solving the problem. In these cases, ask the human resources office if someone from their office can step in and mediate the situation. Alternatively, talk with a senior manager who may be able to intervene and settle the dispute diplomatically.

1. Use a word processor such as Microsoft Office Word to open the file C-6.doc provided with your Data Files, and save it as Difficult.doc in the location where you store your Data Files

2. Read the contents of Difficult.doc, which describe a group in conflict

3. Identify ways to deal with the difficult team member

4. Save and close Difficult.doc, then submit it to your instructor as requested

FIGURE C-9: Unresolved conflicts create larger problems

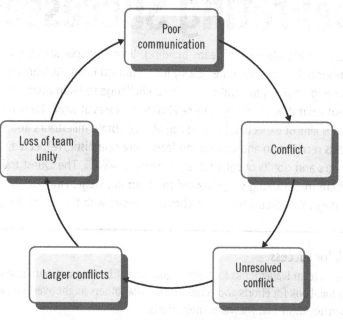

Poor communication (not establishing clear expectations) increases the chances for conflict. Conflicts that linger become unresolved and can grow into larger conflicts that affect more people. Ultimately, they threaten team unity.

TABLE C-6: Dealing with difficult team members do's and don'ts

guideline	do	don't
Prepare for conflict	• Define expectations for the team at the first team meeting • Refer to the team ground rules during conflicts • Learn about the possible roots of a problem • Encourage steady team leadership	**Don't** respond to conflict by immediately treating the symptoms
Respond to conflict	• Work with the team leader to respond to problems directly • Identify inappropriate behaviors • Ask people in conflict how they might resolve their problem • Stay calm and objective • Ask for help from others if the difficulty continues	• **Don't** let a problem escalate by ignoring it • **Don't** attack a person; suggest how to improve their behavior

Guidelines for settling disagreements

Although conflict in teams is inevitable, it can still cause long-term problems that prevent a team from being successful. Howard Guttman, principal of Guttman Development Strategies, offers the following advice for teams handling a difficult team member: "Give them two options: confront the conflict and handle it, or let it go." Letting go can be difficult if your disagreement is rooted in your values or pride. Team leaders should set an example and address conflicts immediately. "As soon as I notice something," says Morris Shechtman of the Shechtman Group, "I get it on the table and address it directly. You want a feedback-rich environment where it is each team member's responsibility to bring up what bothers them." Steven Robbins, an executive coach, suggests a practical way to prevent the conflict from getting too personal. "Put the items [being discussed] on a whiteboard and place team members in a semicircle around it so that they are allied against the conflict." Shechtman also emphasizes personal relationships in teams to increase trust, which often helps to prevent conflict. For example, team members can quickly provide personal and professional updates at the beginning of each team meeting. "This builds relationships before the meeting gets into content—it has an amazing effect on the communication that follows," he says.

Source: Kling, Jim, "Tension in Teams," *Harvard Business Review, Guest Blog, http://blogs.hbr.org/hmu/2009/01/tension-in-teams.html,* January 14, 2009.

Teamwork

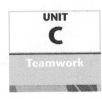

Celebrating Successes

Motivation is a key element of team building. When people are motivated and enthusiastic about a group's mission, they evolve more quickly into a unified team. As teams move ahead with their responsibilities, finding ongoing motivation can be a challenge to team members. One way to help people feel good about what they are doing is to celebrate successes at work. Having a celebration when a project is completed is almost expected, but you can also celebrate milestones and intermediate successes. A team that expects recognition and celebration feels more optimistic, respected, and valued. Table C-7 summarizes the do's and don'ts of celebrating successes. The Quest training guide team seems to be moving from the storming stage toward the norming stage. Figure C-10 shows behaviors typical in the norming stage. You discuss how to celebrate successes with the rest of the team.

ESSENTIAL ELEMENTS

> **QUICK TIP**
> Be generous with your compliments even if you aren't the team leader.

1. Look for success
A skilled team leader looks for what is going right in a team. Compliment people when they are doing a good job. Look for efforts and achievements that others might overlook, and comment on them. Let your teammates know that you value their efforts.

2. Create a forum for sharing accomplishments
Use team meetings to talk about team successes. Let people publicly take credit for their accomplishments. A positive way to start team meetings is by having people briefly talk about their recent successes and achievements. Not only does this provide important recognition, but it also motivates people to do more so they can take credit for achievements in the future.

3. Probe for good news
Some team members enthusiastically share their accomplishments with others. However, others may not be as open with their success. Some people are modest or minimize their accomplishments. Encourage your teammates to share their good news. If they are hesitant, ask whether you can outline what they achieved. Publish news of your team's success in the company blog or newsletter.

> **QUICK TIP**
> Save the social events for truly special occasions.

4. Celebrate by socializing
Social events are an appropriate way to celebrate. When the team reaches an important milestone or works long hours to meet a key deadline, arrange to get together as a group for lunch, dinner, or after work. Even bringing unexpected food or other gifts to work can have a positive effect if people know that you brought them as a way to celebrate their accomplishments.

5. Involve senior management
Team members appreciate the recognition you give them, but it's also important they feel their efforts are valued by the company and others outside the team. When celebrating a key milestone or success, arrange for some senior managers to attend. Ask them in advance if they could make a short speech to recognize and praise the team's efforts. Doing this not only makes the team feel that their efforts are valued, it raises the visibility of the team in the eyes of key stakeholders.

YOU TRY IT

1. Use a word processor such as Microsoft Office Word to open the file **C-7.doc** provided with your Data Files, and save it as Celebrate.doc in the location where you store your Data Files
2. Read the contents of Celebrate.doc, which describe a team meeting
3. Identify ways to celebrate the team's successes
4. Save and close Celebrate.doc, then submit it to your instructor as requested

FIGURE C-10: Typical behaviors in the norming stage

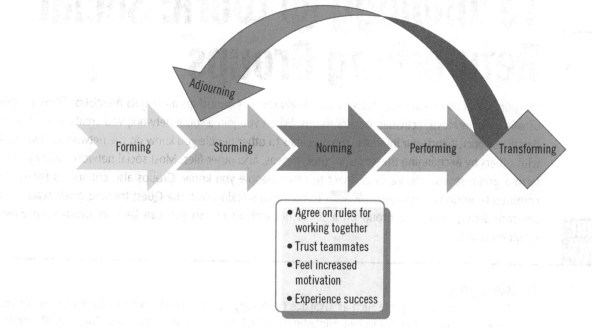

Forming → Storming → Norming → Performing → Transforming

Adjourning

- Agree on rules for working together
- Trust teammates
- Feel increased motivation
- Experience success

TABLE C-7: Celebrating successes do's and don'ts

guideline	do	don't
Talk about successes	• Pay attention to what your teammates are doing and completing • Compliment teammates • Comment specifically about what your teammates are achieving • Talk about team successes during team meetings • Take credit for your accomplishments • Encourage teammates to share good news	• **Don't** bypass a chance to let your teammates know that you value their efforts • **Don't** get caught up with solving problems and conflicts; emphasize the positive too • **Don't** aggressively push a hesitant teammate to share their accomplishments
Celebrate success	• Celebrate team successes with a social event • Reward hard work • Invite managers to your celebration	• **Don't** forget to take time to savor your success • **Don't** celebrate if your team hasn't actually achieved a success or met a milestone

Technology @ Work: Social Networking Groups

The purpose of an online social network is to build social relationships among its members. These people usually share interests, activities, or professions. When you join a social network, you create a profile that describes yourself and your interests. You add links to other people you know on the network and interact with others by exchanging messages, photos, videos, and other files. Most social networks allow you to form a group so you can easily connect to other people you know. Groups also enhance a feeling of community among its members.  To continue working with the Quest training guide team, you are considering creating a group on a social networking site so you can keep in touch even when members travel.

ESSENTIAL ELEMENTS

1. Join a group

On a social networking site such as MySpace (*www.myspace.com*), Facebook (*www.facebook.com*), Twitter (*www.twitter.com*), or LinkedIn (*www.linkedin.com*), look for groups that share your interests. Determine whether and how you can join the group. See Figure C-11.

QUICK TIP

Be careful not to disclose any private or confidential information while online.

2. Create a group

If you want to meet online with people from work, create a group. When you do, you become the owner or manager of the group, which means you can determine who can join. You can also create a group logo and select a group name. Figure C-12 shows the Create a Group page for LinkedIn.

You can also select a group type. For example, on LinkedIn, you can create an alumni group, corporate group, networking group, or professional group, among others. Next, set the access policies to determine who can join the group. For example, you can allow any LinkedIn member to join, or you can approve the people that want to join the group.

3. Start or follow discussions

Most social networks let you start a discussion about a topic. You can post a question or discussion topic, and then read the responses by following the discussion. You can also elect to follow discussions that involve only members of your group. As the group manager, you can stop a discussion by deleting the topic or question that you posted.

YOU TRY IT

1. Open a Web browser such as Microsoft Internet Explorer or Mozilla Firefox, and go to a social networking site mentioned in this lesson

2. Log on or create a free account at the site, if necessary, and then look for a directory of groups

3. Look for a link to create a group, and then click the link to open a page requesting information about the group

4. Press the Print Screen key to take a screen shot of the group directory and the group creation page, open a word-processing program such as Microsoft Word, press Ctrl+V to paste each screen shot in a new document, then send the document to your instructor

FIGURE C-11: Groups directory at LinkedIn

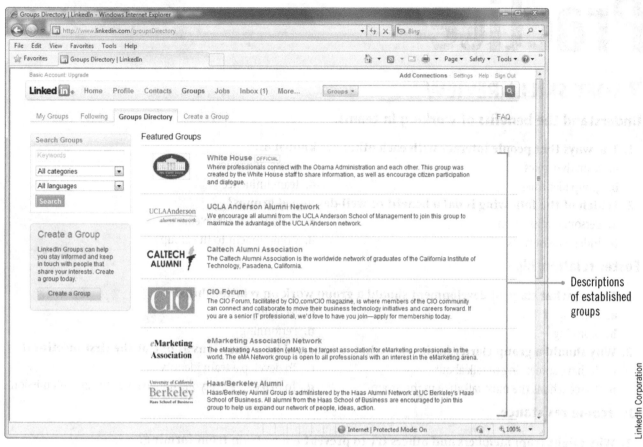

Descriptions
of established
groups

LinkedIn Corporation

FIGURE C-12: Create a Group page for LinkedIn

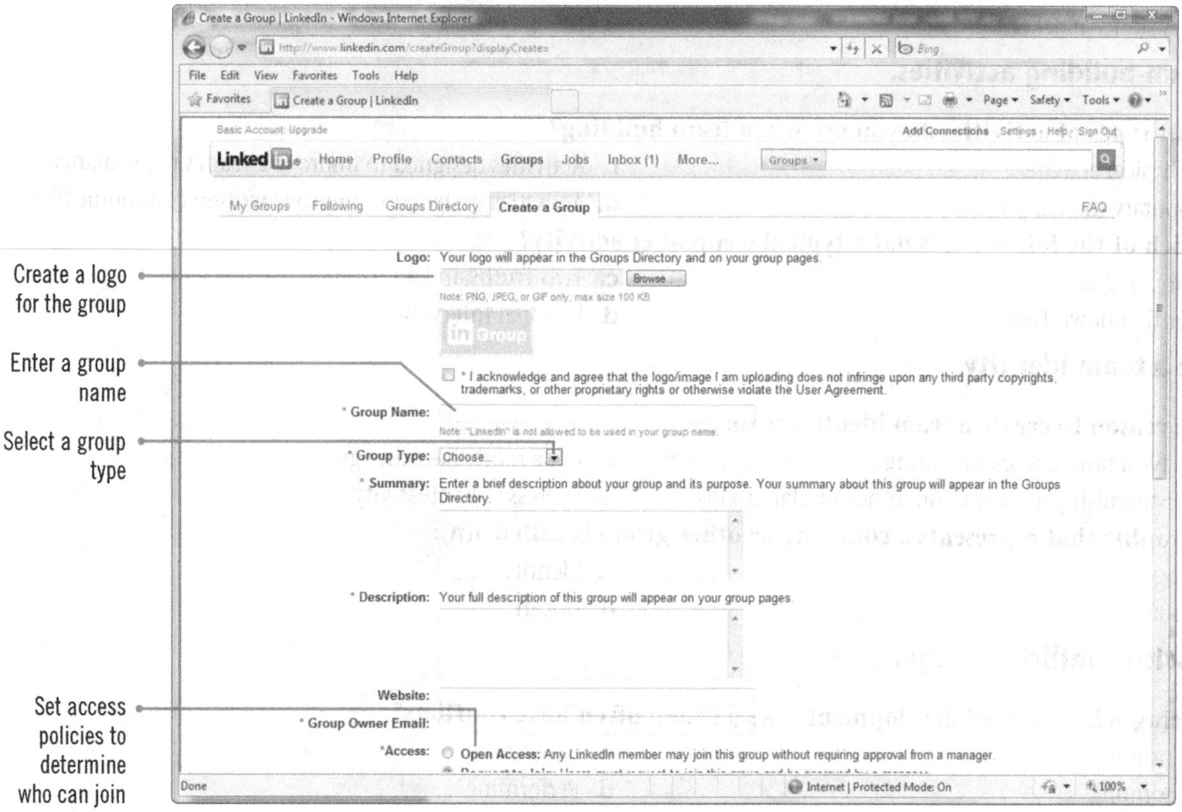

Create a logo
for the group

Enter a group
name

Select a group
type

Set access
policies to
determine
who can join

LinkedIn Corporation

Teamwork

Practice

▼ SOFT SKILLS REVIEW

Understand the benefits of working in teams.

1. The ways that people interact with each other are known as:
   - **a.** team dynamics
   - **b.** group identities
   - **c.** group dynamics
   - **d.** team influence
2. Which of the following is *not* a benefit of well-developed groups?
   - **a.** Personal satisfaction
   - **b.** Independent work
   - **c.** Professional achievement
   - **d.** Commitment to the group

Foster relationships.

1. During what stage of development should a group work on relationships?
   - **a.** Forming
   - **b.** Storming
   - **c.** Norming
   - **d.** Performing
2. Why should a group clarify basic why, what, when, and how questions at one of the first meetings?
   - **a.** To have something to talk about
   - **b.** To see who is the most talkative in the group
   - **c.** To develop a team identity
   - **d.** To make sure everyone understands the group's mission

Overcome resistance.

1. Why might team members and others try to prevent a new team from forming?
   - **a.** New teams mean change
   - **b.** Teams cause only problems for its members
   - **c.** People tend to avoid social interactions
   - **d.** Team-building activities are usually unsuccessful
2. Someone that can inspire or encourage others to change is known as a(n):
   - **a.** agent of morale
   - **b.** resistance blocker
   - **c.** change agent
   - **d.** change manager

Use team-building activities.

1. What types of activities do you use when team building?
   - **a.** Physical activities
   - **b.** Solitary mental puzzles
   - **c.** Activities designed to improve a team's performance
   - **d.** Activities designed to improve written communication
2. Which of the following is *not* a typical icebreaker activity?
   - **a.** Ropes Quiz
   - **b.** Little Known Fact
   - **c.** Two Truths and a Lie
   - **d.** Personal Interview

Create a team identity.

1. One reason to create a team identity is to:
   - **a.** have a task to work on during the first team meeting
   - **b.** distinguish your team from other similar groups
   - **c.** to be more like other groups
   - **d.** express your creativity
2. A graphic that represents a company or other group is called a(n):
   - **a.** logo
   - **b.** brand
   - **c.** identity
   - **d.** slogan

Cope with conflict and ego.

1. During what stage of development does a group often have conflicts?
   - **a.** Forming
   - **b.** Storming
   - **c.** Norming
   - **d.** Performing

2. How can a team leader or member resolve conflict in a group?

a. Focus on the greater good

c. Stay calm and objective

b. Respond directly to unacceptable behavior

d. All of the above

Deal with difficult team members.

1. Which of the following is *not* an effective way to deal with difficult team members?

a. Acknowledge that some team members will always be in conflict

c. Learn more about the conflict

b. Establish clear expectations

d. Clarify who is leading the team

2. Unresolved conflicts can often lead to:

a. loss of team unity

c. the adjourning stage of group development

b. forming a team identity

d. the need for warm-up activities

Celebrate successes.

1. During what stage of development does a group often experience success?

a. Forming

c. Norming

b. Storming

d. Performing

2. Which of the following is *not* an appropriate way to celebrate team success?

a. Announce accomplishments at team meetings

c. Publish news about the success in the company blog

b. Surprise a team member by requesting they speak at a company meeting

d. Organize a social event

Technology @ Work: Social networking groups

1. Most social networks allow you to form a group so you can:

a. connect to other people you know

c. avoid team conflicts

b. complete the performing stage of group development

d. avoid team-building exercises

2. When you create a group at a social networking site, you become the:

a. team leader

c. manager of the group

b. discussion leader

d. profile of the group

▼ CRITICAL THINKING QUESTIONS

1. **Select one group or category that you belong to and identify with. The group can be a team, a club, a professional group, or a class. Discuss the importance of this group in your life. What does membership in this group mean to you? How does it contribute to your social or professional identity?**

2. **What are the potential benefits of being a member of a team? What rewards do teams provide? What drawbacks or costs do they create?**

3. **Do you think it's worthwhile to spend time in group meetings conducting team-building exercises such as Two Truths and a Lie? Have you participated in a group that used different team-building exercises? Describe how effective you found these exercises.**

4. **People who study group dynamics say that conflict is normal and even necessary so that the group can evolve into a team. Do you agree or disagree?**

5. **This unit describes the advantages of creating a team identity. Do you think an identity poses any disadvantages for the team? If so, what are they?**

▼ INDEPENDENT CHALLENGE 1

You work as an administrative assistant to Joanne Burton at Newberry Heating & Cooling, a contracting company in Columbus, Ohio. Joanne assigned you to the Customer Service team. She prepared a few notes for one of the first meetings of the team. She suggests that you answer the questions shown in Figure C-13.

FIGURE C-13

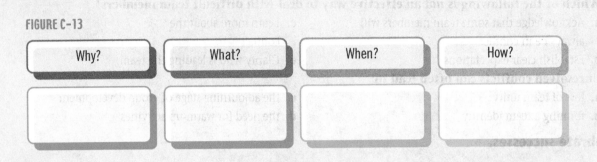

a. Use word-processing software such as Microsoft Office Word to open the file **C-8.doc** provided with your Data Files, and save it as **CS Team.doc** in the location where you store your Data Files.

b. Use presentation software such as Microsoft Office PowerPoint to open the file **C-9.ppt** provided with your Data Files, and save it as **Basic Questions.ppt** in the location where you store your Data Files.

c. Complete the list of questions in Basic Questions.ppt based on the notes in CS Team.doc.

d. Submit the files to your instructor as requested.

▼ INDEPENDENT CHALLENGE 2

You work with George Lambert at a company called PT at Home. The company provides physical therapy services to people in their homes. George assigned you to a team that is working to design, test, and build a new piece of exercise equipment for PT at Home clients. He wants you to create a team identity by selecting a team logo. See Figure C-14.

FIGURE C-14

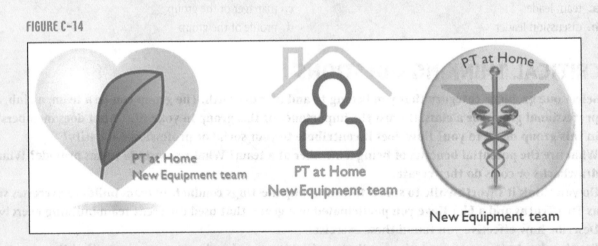

a. Use word-processing software such as Microsoft Office Word to open the file **C-10.doc** provided with your Data Files, and save it as **Logo.doc** in the location where you store your Data Files.

b. Read the description of the PT at Home New Equipment team, and then select a logo from those shown in Figure C-14. In Logo.doc, explain why you selected that particular logo for the team.

c. Submit the document to your instructor as requested.

▼ REAL LIFE INDEPENDENT CHALLENGE

To be a more effective team member, analyze the groups you belong to and how you participate in them by answering the following questions:

  a. Which groups to you belong to? List as many as possible, including groups such as your family, classes, clubs, sports teams, and social organizations.
  b. Which group has changed the most over time? Describe the changes.
  c. Have any of these groups evolved into a team? If so, describe this process. If not, explain why it has not developed into a team.
  d. Which group has influenced you the most? Describe how the group influences you.

▼ TEAM CHALLENGE

You are working for Liz Montoya at Peachtree Landscapers, a landscaping company in Atlanta, Georgia. Liz assigned you to a work team responsible for business customers. She wants your team to discuss each landscaping contract for business customers, suggest ways to better serve those customers, and solve landscaping problems. She suggests that the team should get acquainted by performing a team-building exercise.

  a. Working independently, research *team-building exercise* online or at a library.
  b. Working with your group, select one team-building exercise described in this unit. Then perform the exercise as a group.
  c. Still working with your group, select one team-building exercise that you and your teammates researched. Then perform the exercise as a group.

▼ BE THE CRITIC

You are working for a Web design company that creates Web sites for businesses. You are assigned to the New Technology team, which is supposed to keep up with the latest tools for Web site design and review innovative Web sites. Tyrell Sanders, the team leader, sketches the first three stages of group development for the New Technology team. He also lists the group activities that are typical for each stage. See Figure C-15. Review Tyrell's sketch, and then create a list of suggestions to correct the stages.

FIGURE C-15

Storming

- Avoid conflict
- Share personal information
- Trust teammates
- Have trouble working on tasks

Forming

- Get acquainted
- Feel increased motivation
- Resolve conflicts
- Work hard on team tasks

Norming

- Agree on rules for working together
- Confront people
- Feel frustrated
- Experience success

Leading a Team

Throughout your career, you will work as part of a team. Whether you are collaborating with other students to complete a class project or with other professionals to build a new product, teamwork will be a regular part of your working life. Often, you will be a team member focusing on your assigned tasks. However, as you develop experience and a reputation for effective teamwork, your organization will probably ask you to lead a team. In this unit, you will learn what it takes to be a team leader, how leading a team can contribute to your career, and how to be effective in this role. You recently started working with a new team at Quest Specialty Travel that is responsible for creating a training guide for new employees. Don Novak, the head of the Chicago branch office, and your teammates are nominating you to lead the training guide team. You need to learn more about team leadership before you can decide whether to accept their invitation to lead the team.

OBJECTIVES

Pursue team leadership

Prepare to be a team leader

Get started with your team

Take a project management approach

Manage a team diplomatically

Manage up

Be sensitive to intangibles

Conclude team activities

Pursuing Team Leadership

Some professionals plan careers so they have the same types of responsibilities in each job. Other professionals seek challenges in an effort to grow in their fields. In many industries and organizations, the path to promotion includes positions where you supervise the work of other people. One of the best ways to start supervising or managing others is leading a team. The skills you develop as a team leader help you become an effective manager and serve you well throughout your career. However, not everyone is well suited to be a team leader. If you want to pursue team leadership as part of your career plan, start by assessing yourself. Before you accept the assignment to lead the training guide team, Don Novak encourages you to consider how well suited you are to team leadership.

DETAILS

Before leading a team or workgroup, answer the following questions:

- **Is managing others part of your career plan?**
  No matter what you do professionally, you should create and follow a career plan. This plan should outline what you want to do and the types of jobs you will seek throughout your career. If you eventually want to work as a manager, team leadership is an excellent way to prepare. Directing a team helps you develop interpersonal and management skills. See Figure D-1. If you are a successful team leader, you make yourself more visible to the decision makers in your organization.

- **Are you ready to take on additional responsibilities?**
  One of the biggest differences between being a team member and the team leader is that the leader shoulders most of the responsibility. When you are in charge of a group of people, you must attend to your own tasks, manage the work of others, and solve the team's problems. If you are looking for new challenges and are comfortable accepting responsibility, you are probably ready for team leadership.

- **Do you enjoy supporting, teaching, and helping others?**
  Would you rather focus on tasks or interact with other people? An effective team leader does both well, but being able to work with, guide, motivate, and help others is especially important. As a team leader, you accomplish goals through the efforts of your team. Your role is to provide direction, encouragement, and support. See Figure D-2.

- **Do you have a reputation for excellence in your area of expertise?**
  The least-talented person in the company is rarely promoted to supervise a team. To earn the respect of others, you must be good at what you do and have a history of accomplishments. If your career path involves team leadership and management, start now to develop a reputation of excellence.

- **What are your motivations for leading a team?**
  As you consider whether a leadership role suits you, analyze your motivations. If you are motivated by ego (you want others to think you are better than your teammates), a desire to be the boss, or just to make more money, you will likely be dissatisfied. Being a team leader is not a position of power. Pay increases, if any, usually do not compensate for the additional time and effort that being a good leader requires. Instead, leading a team can be the first step to positions in management.

FIGURE D-1: Team leadership can lead to management positions

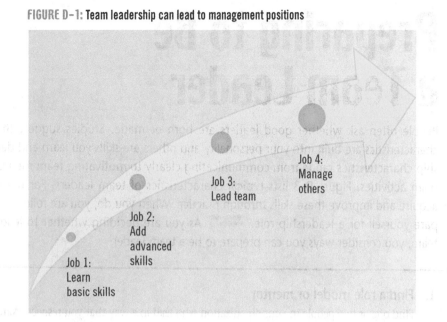

Job 4:
Manage
others

Job 3:
Lead team

Job 2:
Add
advanced
skills

Job 1:
Learn
basic skills

FIGURE D-2: Team leaders must focus on tasks and interact with other people

© Jupiterimages Corporation

Teamwork

Preparing to Be a Team Leader

People often ask whether good leaders are born or made. Studies suggest that some leadership characteristics are built into your personality and others are skills you learn and develop. Team leadership characteristics range from communicating clearly to motivating team members and organizing team activities. Figure D-3 lists typical characteristics of team leaders. For the most part, you can acquire and improve these skills through practice. When you do, you are following basic steps to prepare yourself for a leadership role. █████ As you are deciding whether to lead the training guide team, you consider ways you can prepare to be a team leader.

ESSENTIAL ELEMENTS

1. Find a role model or mentor

Find one or two people in your organization who lead in a way that you respect. Watch how they plan and execute projects and deal with the people on their teams. Pay attention to how they manage difficult situations and personalities. Adapt their best practices for yourself.

2. Volunteer for projects and team assignments

Most companies have a regular stream of projects, committees, activities, and assignments that you can volunteer for. Because they might not be well publicized, be sure to let your manager and others know about your interest. Showing a strong desire to be part of a team makes you an attractive choice when staffing decisions are discussed.

> **QUICK TIP**
> Be sure you know who might cause problems and would be best to avoid if possible.

3. Learn the politics of your organization

You should know the key decision makers in your company, such as who controls the budgets and other important resources. Be a careful and quiet observer. Pay close attention in meetings, hallway interactions, and casual discussions. Try to identify people in the organization who can help support you and your team's efforts. Look and act the way other leaders in your company do. See Figure D-4.

> **QUICK TIP**
> Companies often have budgets for training courses and workshops.

4. Seek training opportunities

Companies frequently offer training sessions for their employees. These courses and workshops are good ways to continue your education. Check with your human resources department or your manager to learn about training opportunities at your company.

5. Identify your own weaknesses and try to strengthen them

Evaluate your strengths and weaknesses. Then identify how you can overcome the weaknesses and build on your strengths. For example, perhaps you have limited experience with budgets, scheduling, report writing, or presentations. Buy some books or take a class at your local college to help round out your skills.

YOU TRY IT

1. Use a word processor such as Microsoft Office Word to open the file D-1.doc provided with your Data Files, and save it as Prepare.doc in the location where you store your Data Files

2. Read the contents of Prepare.doc, which describe a newly formed team

3. Identify how the employee can prepare to be a team leader

4. Save and close Prepare.doc, then submit it to your instructor as requested

FIGURE D-3: Leadership skills

Organization skills
- Define and state team expectations and objectives
- Set deadlines and create schedules
- Balance people and work

Management skills
- Create an identity for the team
- Use strengths of team members to meet goals
- Present team needs to company
- Present company needs to team

People skills
- Communicate frequently with team members
- Motivate others to meet goals
- Build trust among team members
- Listen actively and express ideas clearly

FIGURE D-4: Look and act the part of a leader

© Jupiterimages Corporation

Traits of inspirational leaders

In a recent article in *BusinessWeek*, Alaina Love defines the differences between typical business leaders and inspirational ones. She says, "Inspirational leaders focus unrelentingly on tapping the right people for each job and helping others determine where they can be their best." She identifies 10 traits of inspirational leaders:

1. Authentic rather than phony
2. Reliable rather than erratic
3. Anchored rather than disconnected
4. Optimistic rather than pessimistic
5. Self-aware rather than unconscious
6. Driven by purpose and passion rather than power and fear
7. Inclusive rather than divisive
8. Focused on others rather than self-focused
9. Respectful rather than manipulative
10. Able to foster other leaders rather than demanding followers

Source: Love, Alaina, "You Can Lead. But Can You Inspire?" *BusinessWeek*, December 22, 2009.

Getting Started with Your Team

Congratulations! Your manager just assigned you to direct a new team on an important project. It's natural to be excited and nervous when you are promoted to a new position or given a new assignment. Because others in your organization will be watching as you begin, be sure to start working with your team effectively from the first meeting. Table D-1 lists the do's and don'ts for getting started with your team. After you accept the assignment to lead the Quest training guide team, you focus on how to get off to a good start.

ESSENTIAL ELEMENTS

1. Keep your feet on the ground

Often, new managers are eager to seize control, fix problems, and establish themselves in their position. However, introducing too many changes at once can be threatening to your team and to other managers. Spend most of your first few weeks on relationship-building activities. See Figure D-5.

2. Get to know your team

Quickly connect with your team members and get to know them on a personal and professional level. Learn everyone's names and regularly use them in conversation. Get to know the skills your team members bring to the team and what motivates them. People respond better to leaders that they know, understand, and respect.

QUICK TIP

Develop a delegation habit, which means you assign tasks to others rather than complete them yourself.

3. Assign tasks to team members

When you are a team member, you are usually responsible for your own work. As a leader, you need to change this focus and delegate tasks and responsibilities to your team. Instead of completing a task yourself, ask yourself who would be the best team member to handle it.

4. Set the example you want others to follow

Your team members look to learn how you want them to work and behave. Set a good example for others to follow. For example, if you value punctuality, always be on time to work, meetings, and other appointments. Your actions will always speak louder than any instructions you may give. Don't confuse your team members by expecting one thing and doing another.

QUICK TIP

If you start feeling burned out, take a personal day off to recharge and relax.

5. Pace yourself

A new assignment can boost your energy and enthusiasm. New managers often push themselves to work long days at a hectic pace. They want to accomplish as much as they can and impress their superiors. It's easy to overdo it and suffer burnout. Pace yourself by sticking to regular work hours, taking a lunch break every day, and using a personal calendar to help manage your time. Don't make a habit of working nights or weekends unless a key deadline is looming.

YOU TRY IT

1. Use a word processor such as Microsoft Office Word to open the file D-2.doc provided with your Data Files, and save it as Getting Started.doc in the location where you store your Data Files

2. Read the contents of Getting Started.doc, which describe a newly formed team

3. Identify how the leader can start building a team

4. Save and close Getting Started.doc, then submit it to your instructor as requested

FIGURE D-5: Relationship-building activities

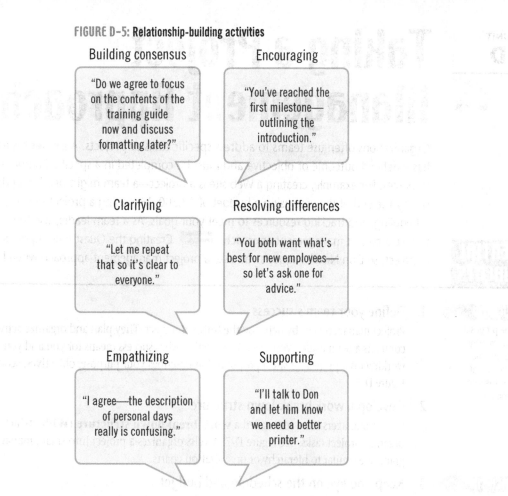

Building consensus

"Do we agree to focus on the contents of the training guide now and discuss formatting later?"

Encouraging

"You've reached the first milestone— outlining the introduction."

Clarifying

"Let me repeat that so it's clear to everyone."

Resolving differences

"You both want what's best for new employees— so let's ask one for advice."

Empathizing

"I agree—the description of personal days really is confusing."

Supporting

"I'll talk to Don and let him know we need a better printer."

TABLE D-1: Getting started with your team do's and don'ts

guideline	do	don't
Get to know your team	• Learn the names of everyone on your team • Establish a relationship with each team member • Spend time during the first few weeks on team-building activities	• **Don't** rush to take control, fix problems, and establish yourself as leader • **Don't** introduce too many changes at once
Assign tasks to team members	• Delegate tasks and responsibilities to your team • For each task, consider who on the team can best handle the task	**Don't** complete team tasks yourself
Set an example	• Work and behave the way you want the team to work and behave • Pace yourself and your team by sticking to regular work hours	• **Don't** expect team members to attend meetings on time and then show up late for meetings • **Don't** make a habit of working nights and weekends

Taking a Project Management Approach

Organizations often use teams to address specific tasks or projects. A **project** is a temporary effort that has a defined outcome or objective and must be completed in a specified amount of time using certain resources. For example, creating a Web site is a project—a team might need to update the company Web site by the end of the year using a budget of $2,500. Managing a project involves planning, organizing, scheduling, and tracking resources to meet your goals. As a team leader, use the guidelines in this lesson to take a project management approach. Creating the Quest training guide for new employees is a project, so Don Novak suggests you take a project management approach when leading the team.

ESSENTIAL ELEMENTS

1. Define your team's success

Project managers start by defining the finished project. They plan and organize activities to match that outcome. As a team leader, you should also define what success means for you and your group. Before you start working on a project, create a proposal that describes your purpose, objectives, scope, and deliverables. See Figure D-6.

2. Develop a work breakdown structure

Project managers use a tool called a **work breakdown structure (WBS)**, which is a diagram you use to organize project tasks. See Figure D-7. A WBS organizes a project into small, manageable pieces. These diagrams are similar to hierarchy or organization charts.

3. Keep one eye on the schedule and budget

In addition to the project goals, focus on the schedule and the budget. Be sure you understand what your budget is before you begin a project. Estimate your expenses and talk to your manager if you think they will exceed your budget. During the project, monitor your expenses carefully. Most companies see missing important deadlines or having to ask for more money as signs of trouble or failure.

4. Develop and use a communication plan

Skilled project managers develop communication plans to keep other managers and important stakeholders informed about their projects. Communication plans include writing progress reports, giving status updates at company meetings, and meeting with managers to keep them informed.

5. Practice risk management

Project managers anticipate risks and plan for problems. If a shipment is late, a key employee gets sick, the weather is uncooperative, or disaster strikes, you should plan how to keep your project moving forward. Think of risks as what-ifs—what if we can't find an inexpensive source for graphics? What if the training guide file is too big to post on the Web site? Then find acceptable alternatives.

YOU TRY IT

1. Use a word processor such as Microsoft Office Word to open the file D-3.doc provided with your Data Files, and save it as Project.doc in the location where you store your Data Files

2. Read the contents of Project.doc, which describe a team's purpose and activities

3. Organize the activities into a project management chart

4. Save and close Project.doc, then submit it to your instructor as requested

FIGURE D-6: Project proposal

> ### Training Guide Project Proposal
>
> #### Purpose
> To provide guidelines for new employees at Quest Specialty Travel
>
> #### Objectives
> - To collect all the information a new employee needs to know
> - To describe the policies for Quest employees
> - To outline the steps for completing typical procedures
>
> #### Scope
> This training guide is designed for all new employees of Quest Specialty Travel, including those at all of its branch offices.
>
> #### Deliverables
> - Printed and bound 32-page training guide
> - Electronic files

FIGURE D-7: Work breakdown structure

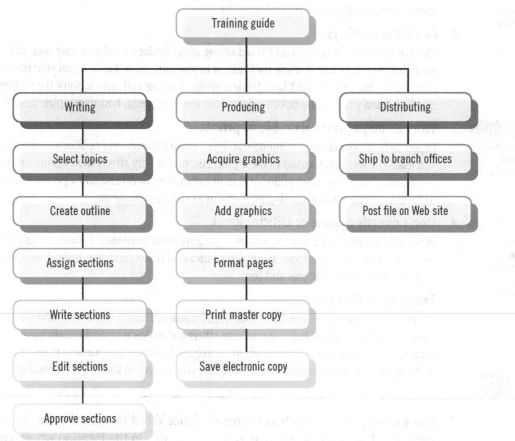

Managing a Team Diplomatically

People often use the words *authority* and *responsibility* when talking about management. As a team leader, your authority or power over people and situations is probably limited. However, your responsibility for those same people and situations is significant. Managing a team generally requires a soft touch, good persuasion skills, and a diplomatic approach. Providing the group with lots of encouragement, support, and understanding pays off when you need your team's support for a difficult task. Table D-2 outlines the do's and don'ts for managing a team diplomatically. Now that the Quest training guide team is starting to work on the guide, you want to make sure you are leading the team diplomatically.

ESSENTIAL ELEMENTS

QUICK TIP

Being available to your team enhances your visibility, improves communication, and creates a positive working relationship.

1. Maintain high visibility

If team members don't feel comfortable approaching their leader, progress will be slow and problems will remain unsolved. Keep an open-door policy and manage by walking around. Encourage your team to come to you with questions, ideas, and concerns. Now your focus shifts from building relationships to helping team members complete tasks. See Figure D-8.

2. Avoid the monkeys

Monkey management is based on the old saying about *having a monkey on your back*. In business, a monkey is an idea, project, or task that you try to assign to someone else but ends up on your back. In most cases, the other person claims they don't have the knowledge, time, or authority to solve the problem. To avoid these monkeys when you delegate tasks, be clear about the assignment, how to complete it, and when it is due.

QUICK TIP

Saving face means to maintain a good image or reputation.

3. Work through personal problems privately

Expect to have your share of misunderstandings, sharp differences of opinions, and conflict with any team you lead. The way you respond to these problems profoundly affects their resolution. If you are having a conflict with someone, don't confront him or her in front of others. Allow people to save face by meeting with them privately and discussing problems in a calm, reasonable way.

QUICK TIP

Be aware of your body language. Grimacing or rolling your eyes can send powerful messages.

4. Don't directly oppose or criticize ideas

When you are the leader, your words and opinions often have more influence than those of other team members. Never directly oppose or criticize an idea that someone shares. Instead, encourage the discussion, and let others identify the pros and cons.

5. Praise more than correct

Don't overlook the value of praising your team members. Praise is one of the most effective rewards a team leader can provide. Praise helps to motivate others and makes it easier for team members to accept corrections you give. When you praise people more frequently than you reprimand them, they will be more open and responsive to your suggestions knowing that you appreciate and respect them and their work.

YOU TRY IT

1. Use a word processor such as Microsoft Office Word to open the file D-4.doc provided with your Data Files, and save it as Managing.doc in the location where you store your Data Files

2. Read the contents of Managing.doc, which describe a team

3. Identify how the team leader can manage more diplomatically

4. Save and close Managing.doc, then submit it to your instructor as requested

FIGURE D-8: Task management activities

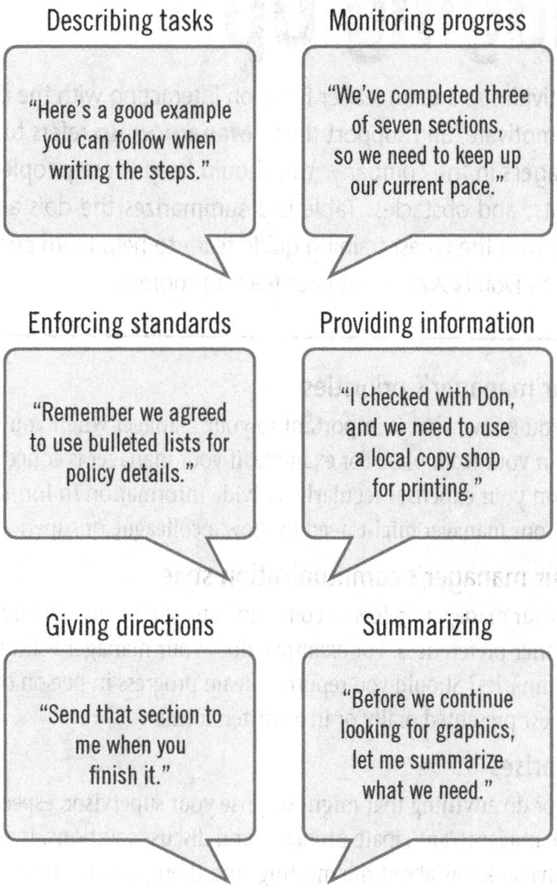

Describing tasks

"Here's a good example you can follow when writing the steps."

Monitoring progress

"We've completed three of seven sections, so we need to keep up our current pace."

Enforcing standards

"Remember we agreed to use bulleted lists for policy details."

Providing information

"I checked with Don, and we need to use a local copy shop for printing."

Giving directions

"Send that section to me when you finish it."

Summarizing

"Before we continue looking for graphics, let me summarize what we need."

TABLE D-2: Managing a team diplomatically do's and don'ts

guideline	do	don't
Maintain visibility	• Encourage team members to approach you when they need help • Manage by walking around • Work on tasks with team members	• **Don't** hide behind a closed door • **Don't** wait for team members to come to you
Communicate clearly	• Clearly define each assignment to team members • Discuss how to complete each team assignment • Identify when the assignment is due and what exactly is requested • Work through misunderstandings and other personal conflicts privately	• **Don't** end up completing a task you assigned to a team member • **Don't** confront team members in public when you need to discuss a personal conflict
Praise efforts	• Praise more often than you correct • Remember that as a team leader, your reactions and opinions are influential • Encourage team members to discuss pros and cons	• **Don't** directly oppose or criticize ideas from team members • **Don't** wait to correct or reprimand team members; find something to praise

UNIT
D
Teamwork

Managing Up

Most of your activities as a team leader focus on interacting with the other members of the team and how you can direct, motivate, and support them. **Managing up** refers to working with your direct supervisor and other managers in the company. You should keep these people informed about the team's efforts, accomplishments, and obstacles. Table D-3 summarizes the do's and don'ts of managing up. Besides working with the Quest training guide team to help them complete their tasks, you need to manage up and talk to Don Novak about your team's progress.

ESSENTIAL ELEMENTS

1. Know your manager's priorities

Make sure you know what is important to your manager when you start working with your team. Include those goals in your work plan. For example, if your manager is concerned about staying within budget, plan and report on your expenses regularly. Provide information in formats that are easy to access, such as lists and tables. Your manager might need to show a colleague or superior that your team is successful.

QUICK TIP

Anticipate when your manager needs more information about your team, and provide it before he or she requests it.

2. Adopt your manager's communication style

Learn how your manager prefers to communicate, such as by e-mail or face to face. Ask your manager about his or her other preferences. For example, does your manager want frequent, detailed information or only periodic summaries? Should you report on team progress in person or in a written format? Would the information be best presented orally or in a written format?

3. Avoid surprises

Do not say or do anything that might surprise your supervisor, especially in public. Communicate regularly with your manager to anticipate problems and discuss solutions. If another manager asks to meet with you, let your manager know about the meeting, and then provide updates on the results.

4. Deliver bad news in person

Your team will occasionally make mistakes. An unexpected problem might affect the team and its project. When you need to deliver bad news to your manager, deliver it in person. Don't send an e-mail message or memo to avoid an uncomfortable discussion. If you are in a different location, call your manager. Choose a time when you won't inconvenience your manager, but don't wait too long. You don't want your boss to learn about the bad news from someone else.

5. Package solutions with problems

When you have to communicate a problem to your manager, bundle a proposed solution with it. Deliver them together. Figure D-9 illustrates a conversation that provides solutions along with a problem.

YOU TRY IT

1. Use a word processor such as Microsoft Office Word to open the file D-5.doc provided with your Data Files, and save it as Supervisor.doc in the location where you store your Data Files

2. Read the contents of Supervisor.doc, which describe a team

3. Identify how the team leader can keep the supervisor informed more effectively

4. Save and close Supervisor.doc, then submit it to your instructor as requested

FIGURE D-9: Packaging solutions with problems

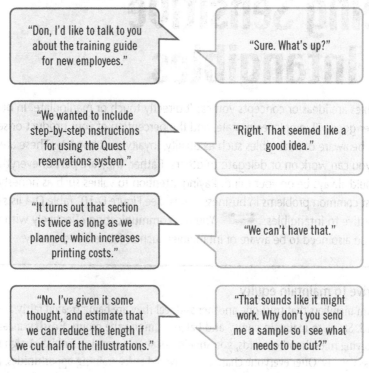

"Don, I'd like to talk to you about the training guide for new employees."

"Sure. What's up?"

"We wanted to include step-by-step instructions for using the Quest reservations system."

"Right. That seemed like a good idea."

"It turns out that section is twice as long as we planned, which increases printing costs."

"We can't have that."

"No. I've given it some thought, and estimate that we can reduce the length if we cut half of the illustrations."

"That sounds like it might work. Why don't you send me a sample so I see what needs to be cut?"

TABLE D-3: Managing up do's and don'ts

guideline	do	don't
Know your manager	• Learn what matters to your manager • Include your manager's goals in your work plan • Provide your manager with information about your team's progress • Communicate with your manager according to his or her preferences	• **Don't** assume your manager knows what your team is doing • **Don't** provide details when your manager prefers overviews or summaries
Keep in touch with your manager	• Anticipate problems and discuss how to avoid or solve them • Keep your manager informed about meetings you have with his or her superiors • Identify when the assignment is due and what exactly is requested • Deliver bad news to your manager in person • Provide solutions when you present problems	• **Don't** surprise your manager with unexpected information, especially in public • **Don't** try to solve a problem by discussing it with someone more senior than your manager • **Don't** send an electronic message to your manager to avoid an uncomfortable discussion • **Don't** ask a team member to deliver bad news to your manager • **Don't** wait too long to deliver bad news

Being Sensitive to Intangibles

Intangibles are ideas or concepts you can't directly touch or manipulate. In business, intangibles include customer goodwill, employee morale, and the perception of your product or service. When working with a team, be aware of intangibles such as quality, loyalty, and honesty. These are not direct tasks or assignments you can work on or delegate to others. Rather, they are part of everything you do with the team and should always be on your mind. Paying attention to values such as honesty and integrity can prevent the most common problems in business teams. See Figure D-10. Table D-4 lists the do's and don'ts for being sensitive to intangibles. You are communicating effectively with your team and your managers. You also need to be aware of intangibles such as fairness and quality.

1. **Strive to maintain equity**

   Team members that trust one another and feel they are being treated fairly are motivated to keep working hard. Strive to maintain equity and balance among the group. **Equity** means fairness, especially when applying rules. In other words, you should not show favoritism or bias. Assign the popular and the difficult tasks equally. Offer everyone chances for favored tasks, training opportunities, and other perks.

2. **Make professional information transparent**

   Business teams need information to do their jobs effectively. Make sure your communication style doesn't create a **knowledge gap** in the team. A knowledge gap appears when you regularly talk to and share information with certain people but not others. Except for relating personal or confidential information, be open and transparent with the team. In this context, **transparent** describes information that anyone can access.

3. **Focus on quality**

   The quality of the work that you and your team produce is as important as meeting goals and deadlines. Remind your team that quality matters. If they do all or most of their tasks well, they will be pleased and proud of the final product.

4. **Demonstrate loyalty**

   When you lead a team, it should be your first priority. Your job is to make the team look good, not the other way around. Give credit where it's due, and praise the efforts of your team whenever you can. If team members know you are loyal to them, they will reciprocate and be loyal to you.

5. **Be honest and ethical**

   Being honest in all your personal and professional dealings is especially important when you are responsible for the work of others. Never take unfair advantage of a situation or someone outside the group. Even if this seems like you are doing something that may help the team, if you are less than ethical about it, your group members will suspect your motives and integrity.

1. Use a word processor such as Microsoft Office Word to open the file D-6.doc provided with your Data Files, and save it as Intangibles.doc in the location where you store your Data Files

2. Read the contents of Intangibles.doc, which describe team interactions

3. Identify which statements address the intangibles of the team

4. Save and close Intangibles.doc, then submit it to your instructor as requested

FIGURE D-10: Preventing common problems in business teams

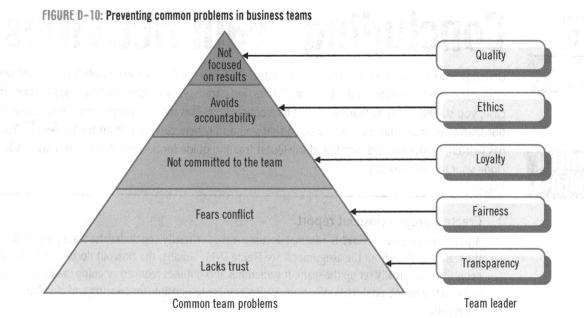

Common team problems (pyramid, bottom to top):
- Lacks trust
- Fears conflict
- Not committed to the team
- Avoids accountability
- Not focused on results

Team leader (top to bottom):
- Quality
- Ethics
- Loyalty
- Fairness
- Transparency

TABLE D-4: Being sensitive to intangibles do's and don'ts

guideline	do	don't
Be fair	• Apply rules fairly to all team members • Assign popular and difficult tasks equally among the team	• **Don't** show favoritism or bias • **Don't** offer rewards and other benefits only to some team members
Be transparent	• Discuss team matters at team meetings • Send updates to the team via e-mail • Include all team members in important discussions and decisions	**Don't** create a knowledge gap in your team
Demonstrate quality, loyalty, and honesty	• Remind yourself and the team to produce quality work • Make the team your first priority • Represent team interests to your supervisor • Be honest and ethical with your team	• **Don't** take credit for success the entire team has earned • **Don't** take advantage of someone outside the group

Concluding Team Activities

Unless you are the chair of a standing committee, your team will either accomplish what it set out to do or disband due to changes in the company's direction, strategy, ownership, or financial situation. In either case, you should bring all team activities to a conclusion. This means completing tasks, resolving questions, and documenting team activities so that you and others can learn from them. Your team has written, produced, and distributed the Quest training guide for new employees. You are ready to conclude your team's activities.

ESSENTIAL ELEMENTS

1. Create a project closeout report

A **project closeout report** is a formal document that officially concludes the team project and releases the team members from the assignment. See Figure D-11. Usually, the closeout document is signed by the people who originally set up the team. It sometimes also outlines required ongoing maintenance or future work on the team's product. As the team leader, you are responsible for creating and circulating the closeout report.

QUICK TIP

Summarize the lessons learned in a report or in a company forum.

2. Document the lessons learned

Organizational memory is the collection of information and specialized knowledge in a company. To document the lessons learned on your team, work with your team to identify what went right, what went wrong, and what people would do differently if they could redo the experience.

3. Ask for feedback

Before you assume that your assignment is complete, check with the stakeholders, the people outside of the team that are involved in your team's project. For example, ask your manager and others for candid feedback about your team's performance. Are they satisfied with what your team accomplished? Do you need to do more before concluding the project?

4. Survey your team

Another way to assess your performance is to survey your team members and ask them about the experience, the process, your leadership, and how they got along with each other. Ask basic questions about team activities and commitment questions about team attitudes. See Figure D-12. Make this an anonymous survey, and don't try to figure out who wrote each response. Instead, use the feedback constructively as you look ahead to your next assignment.

QUICK TIP

Write a personal letter of thanks to each member of your team specifying their contributions.

5. Hold a formal conclusion

You need to have a formal conclusion to signal the end of the team's project. A conclusion can be a team meeting, an offsite event, or a presentation to other people in the company. It can be reserved or festive. Recognize everyone for their contributions as you summarize the team's list of accomplishments. Be sure to answer questions about what might come next for team members or ask managers to answer these questions during the conclusion.

YOU TRY IT

1. Use a word processor such as Microsoft Office Word to open the file D-7.doc provided with your Data Files, and save it as Conclude.doc in the location where you store your Data Files

2. Read the contents of Conclude.doc, which describe the final stage of a team project

3. Identify how the team leader can conclude team activities

4. Save and close Conclude.doc, then submit it to your instructor as requested

FIGURE D-11: Project closeout report

Item	Milestone or deliverable	Due date	Actual date
Project kickoff	M	4/3/13	4/3/13
Draft project plan	D	4/10/13	4/10/13
Approve project plan	D	4/14/13	4/15/13
Write training guide	D	5/28/13	5/28/13
Format training guide	D	6/5/13	6/12/13
Produce training guide	D	6/12/13	6/15/13
Distribute training guide	D	6/15/13	6/16/13
Project completed	M	6/18/13	6/18/13

FIGURE D-12: Questions to ask when surveying your team

Basic questions

- How do you rate your experience working with the team?
- How productive did you find the team meetings?
- How do you rate the results of the team?

Commitment questions

- How interested would you be in working with this team again in the future??
- What do you think contributed to the team's success?
- What do you think contributed to the team's failings?

Technology @ Work: Online Survey Tools

When you want to survey members of your team, you can use online survey tools to take care of the mechanics of creating and administering online surveys. Survey tools such as Survey Monkey (*www.surveymonkey.com*) and Zoomerang (*www.zoomerang.com*) let you use your Web browser to create surveys. Using Survey Monkey, for example, you can select the types of questions you want to ask, customize the survey form, collect responses, and then analyze the results. Team members can then use their Web browsers to complete the surveys.  Now that you are concluding the Quest training guide team, you want to survey the team members so you can learn from the experience. Don Novak suggests you use an online survey tool to create and administer the survey.

ESSENTIAL ELEMENTS

1. **Design the survey**

   Using an online survey tool such as Survey Monkey, you can start by naming the survey and then selecting a theme. The survey shown in Figure D-13 uses the Sea Green theme. Next, you enter each survey question. Select the type of question you want to ask, such as multiple choice with one correct answer, a rating scale, or a short answer question, and then enter the question text. Both Survey Monkey and Zoomerang provide templates to help you create typical types of surveys. Figure D-14 shows a Zoomerang template for a consumer demographics survey.

2. **Select how to collect responses**

   After you create a survey, you need to let team members know it's available. Using Survey Monkey or Zoomerang, you can generate a link that you paste in an e-mail message or Web page. Team members can open the e-mail message or Web page, and then click the link to display the survey in their Web browser. You can also select different ways to collect responses, such as displaying a pop-up window when users visit your Web site. The pop-up window contains the survey or an invitation to complete the survey. To manage the survey on Survey Monkey, you can choose whether to allow multiple responses, set a cutoff date for responses, and add responses collected from printed forms.

3. **Analyze results**

   Online survey tools also collect the responses to your survey, and then analyze the results. For example, Survey Monkey records how many people selected each option for each question on your survey. It also records how many total people answered the question and how many skipped the question. You can also view the responses in different ways, including as a summary or as a detailed list.

YOU TRY IT

1. Open a Web browser such as Microsoft Internet Explorer or Mozilla Firefox, and go to one of the survey Web sites mentioned in this lesson

2. Log on or create a free account at the site, if necessary

3. Create a survey that asks questions about favorite vacation spots by following the instructions provided by the Web site

4. Send a link to the survey to at least three classmates

5. After your classmates complete the survey, analyze the results

6. Press the Print Screen key to take a screen shot of the results page, open a word-processing program such as Microsoft Word, press Ctrl+V to paste each screen shot in a new document, then send the document to your instructor

FIGURE D-13: Creating a survey at Survey Monkey

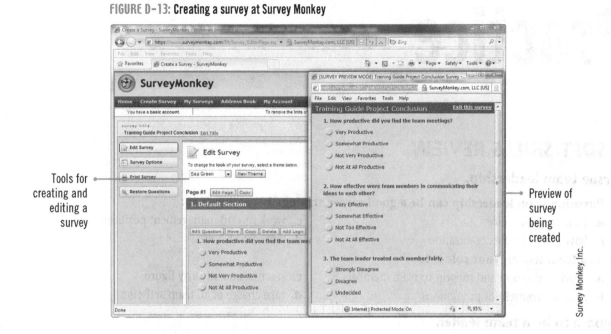

Tools for creating and editing a survey

Preview of survey being created

Survey Monkey Inc.

FIGURE D-14: Zoomerang consumer survey template

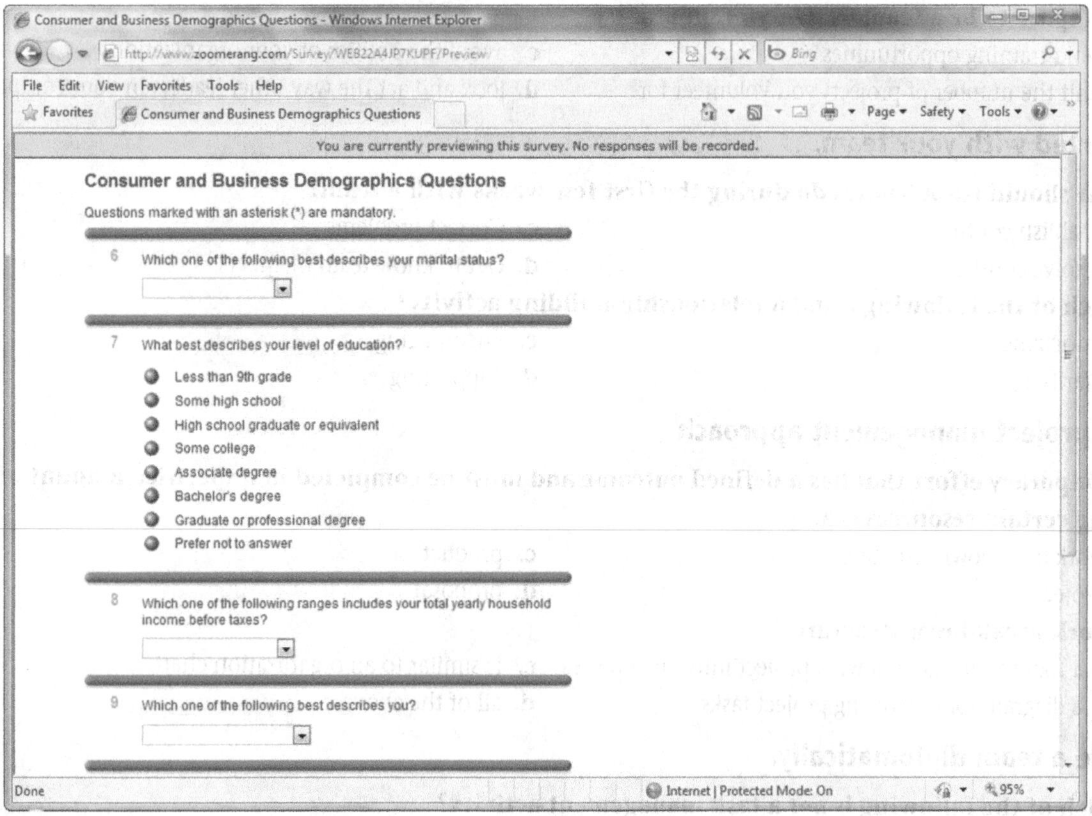

Survey Monkey Inc.

Teamwork

Practice

▼ SOFT SKILLS REVIEW

Pursue team leadership.

1. **Pursuing team leadership can be a good career strategy if you want to:**
   - **a.** increase your salary
   - **b.** have power in the organization
   - **c.** work toward management positions
   - **d.** work fewer hours

2. **As a team leader, your role is to:**
   - **a.** provide direction and support to team members
   - **b.** position yourself for promotions
   - **c.** serve as an authority figure
   - **d.** take charge of all team activities

Prepare to be a team leader.

1. **Which of the following is *not* a skill typically required for a team leader?**
   - **a.** Communicate frequently with team members
   - **b.** Take credit for team accomplishments
   - **c.** Present team needs to company
   - **d.** Set deadlines and create schedules

2. **To prepare to be a team leader, you should:**
   - **a.** avoid training opportunities
   - **b.** limit the number of projects you volunteer for
   - **c.** avoid the politics of your organization
   - **d.** look and act the way other leaders in your company do

Get started with your team.

1. **What should team leaders do during the first few weeks with a team?**
   - **a.** Establish control
   - **b.** Resolve conflicts
   - **c.** Correct problems
   - **d.** Get to know team members

2. **Which of the following is *not* a relationship-building activity?**
   - **a.** Criticizing
   - **b.** Clarifying
   - **c.** Encouraging
   - **d.** Supporting

Take a project management approach.

1. **A temporary effort that has a defined outcome and must be completed in a specified amount of time using certain resources is a:**
   - **a.** work breakdown structure
   - **b.** project
   - **c.** product
   - **d.** proposal

2. **A work breakdown structure:**
   - **a.** is a tool for breaking down a project into small pieces
   - **b.** is a diagram for organizing project tasks
   - **c.** is similar to an organization chart
   - **d.** all of the above

Manage a team diplomatically.

1. **Which of the following is *not* a task management activity?**
   - **a.** Monitoring progress
   - **b.** Building consensus
   - **c.** Enforcing standards
   - **d.** Giving directions

2. **How can you avoid completing a task you delegated to a team member?**
   - **a.** Acknowledge that the team member does not know how to complete the task
   - **b.** Clearly define the task
   - **c.** Explain how to complete the task
   - **d.** Set a due date

Manage up.

1. Managing up means:

 a. to work with your manager and other managers in the company

 b. to show enthusiasm as a team leader

 c. to accept responsibility for your team

 d. to conclude team activities on a high note

2. When you have to communicate a problem to your manager, be sure to:

 a. describe the problem dramatically to grab your manager's attention

 b. bundle a proposed solution with it

 c. avoid accountability

 d. send an e-mail instead of meeting face to face

Be sensitive to intangibles.

1. Which of the following is *not* an intangible you should be sensitive to as a team leader?

 a. quality

 b. loyalty

 c. legality

 d. honesty

2. When you regularly talk to and share information with certain people but not others, you are creating a(n):

 a. honesty gap

 b. intangible gap

 c. sensitivity gap

 d. knowledge gap

Conclude team activities.

1. One way to officially conclude a team project is to:

 a. create a project closeout report

 b. cancel team meetings

 c. create a project proposal

 d. hold a kickoff meeting

2. Why might you survey your team at the end of a project?

 a. To figure out who is critical of the team

 b. To collect feedback for your next assignment

 c. To read praise about your leadership

 d. To hide problems from your manager

Technology @ Work: Online survey tools

1. Which of the following is a task you can perform with an online survey tool?

 a. Create a survey

 b. Collect responses

 c. Analyze results

 d. All of the above

2. After you create an online survey, how do team members complete it?

 a. By using their Web browsers

 b. By printing the survey

 c. By using their e-mail software

 d. By meeting to complete the survey together

▼ CRITICAL THINKING QUESTIONS

1. Suppose you are the leader of a team that needs to complete a project by the end of next week. Half the team wants to require everyone to work through the weekend to complete the project. The other half of the team wants to make working the extra hours voluntary. How do you handle this conflict?

2. You have probably been a member of one or more teams already, whether at school or work. Who was the most effective leader of your teams? What qualities did this leader have that made him or her effective?

3. You are leading a team of eight people who must complete a demanding project. Six of the team members are working hard and producing quality work. The other two team members are often late to team meetings and are not doing as much work as their six teammates. What problems can this combination of behaviors cause? What can you do to solve them?

4. Suppose you are leading a virtual team with members in three locations and time zones in the United States, one location in India, and another in Germany. All the team members speak English, though the nonnative speakers have heavy accents. What challenges does leading this virtual team present for you? How can you overcome them?

▼ CRITICAL THINKING QUESTIONS (CONTINUED)

5. You are the leader of a team updating one of your company's most popular products. You have been careful to keep the team's work private so that your company's competitors do not learn about the changes to the product. However, when one of your team members arrives at work on Monday, she announces that she has accepted a job at your company's major competitor and is giving her two week notice. What do you do?

▼ INDEPENDENT CHALLENGE 1

You work at Newberry Heating & Cooling, a contracting company in Columbus, Ohio. Your manager, Joanne Burton, assigned you to the Customer Service team when you started at Newberry, and she recently asked you to lead the team. Your first assignment is to produce a guide for Customer Service employees. Joanne has already created an outline for the guide and started a basic work breakdown structure diagram. See Figure D-15.

FIGURE D-15

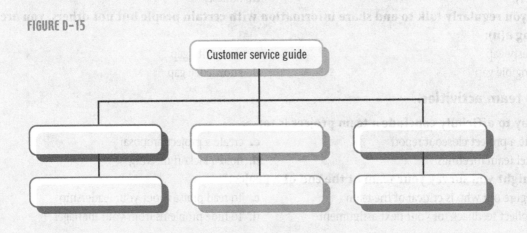

a. Use word-processing software such as Microsoft Office Word to open the file **D-8.doc** provided with your Data Files, and save it as **Guide.doc** in the location where you store your Data Files.

b. Review the contents of Guide.doc, which describe the Customer Service guide.

c. Use presentation software such as Microsoft Office PowerPoint to open the file **D-9.ppt** provided with your Data Files, and save it as **WBS.ppt** in the location where you store your Data Files.

d. Complete the work breakdown structure diagram in WBS.ppt based on the description in Guide.doc.

e. Submit the files to your instructor as requested.

▼ INDEPENDENT CHALLENGE 2

You work with George Lambert at a company called PT at Home, which provides physical therapy services to people in their homes. George assigned you to a team that is working to design, test, and build a new piece of exercise equipment for PT at Home clients. You have been leading the team for the past few months, and are now ready to conclude its activities. George asks you to provide a project closeout report by completing the table shown in Figure D-16.

FIGURE D-16

Item	Milestone or deliverable	Due date	Actual date

a. Use word-processing software such as Microsoft Office Word to open the file **D-10.doc** provided with your Data Files, and save it as **Closeout.doc** in the location where you store your Data Files.

b. Read the description of the PT at Home New Equipment team project, and then complete the table in Closeout.doc.

c. Submit the document to your instructor as requested.

▼ REAL LIFE INDEPENDENT CHALLENGE

To prepare to be a more effective team leader, analyze the leaders of groups you belonged to or are participating in now. Answer the following questions or complete the following activities:

a. List three or four groups you have participated in. Identify the leader of each group.

b. For each leader, list their relationship-building skills and provide an example. Also list their task management skills and provide an example.

c. Next, list the intangibles that each leader emphasized, such as integrity, quality, and loyalty. Provide an example, if possible.

d. Finally, for each team, answer the questions shown in Figure D-12. Your results should reveal excellent team leader traits that you can adopt for yourself.

▼ TEAM CHALLENGE

You are working for Liz Montoya at Peachtree Landscapers, a landscaping company in Atlanta, Georgia. Liz asked you to lead a team designing sustainable gardens for a community college. The project will involve the following tasks:

- Planting a vegetable garden to supply food to the college's restaurants and cafeterias
- Creating a rain garden
- Developing a compost system
- Installing rain barrels
- Setting up a honey bee hive

Complete the following:

a. Working as a group, assign at least one person to each task. Create a form similar to the one shown in Figure D-17. The task each team member should complete is to list the steps necessary to plant a vegetable garden, for example, or to install rain barrels. Complete the first three columns in the form.

b. Working independently, research your task. List the major steps to complete the task. Use a work breakdown structure or other format to list the steps.

c. Provide your task steps to other members of the group.

d. Working with your group, complete the last column in the form.

FIGURE D-17

Task to complete	Team member to complete the task	Date due	Date completed

▼ BE THE CRITIC

You are working for Video Direct, a company in Ann Arbor, Michigan, that creates corporate training videos. You are a member of a team developing videos for a restaurant chain. Over the course of a few meetings, Myra Campbell, the team leader, makes the statements shown in Figure D-18. Review Myra's statements, and then list the statements that build team relationships or help her manage tasks. Also list the statements that do not build team relationships or help Myra manage tasks. (*Note*: Ben is Myra's manager.)

FIGURE D-18

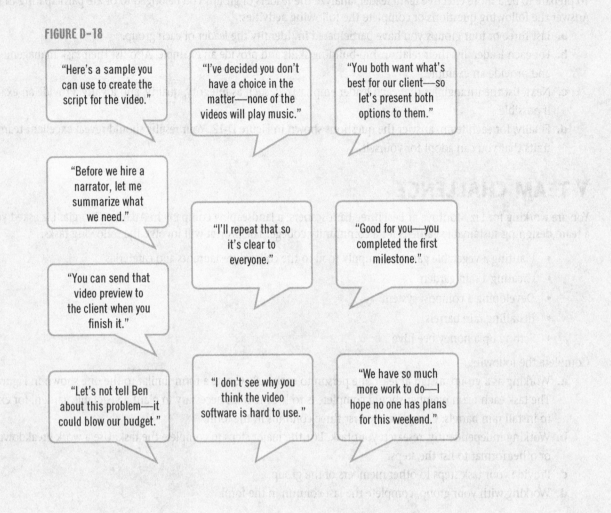

"Here's a sample you can use to create the script for the video."

"I've decided you don't have a choice in the matter—none of the videos will play music."

"You both want what's best for our client—so let's present both options to them."

"Before we hire a narrator, let me summarize what we need."

"I'll repeat that so it's clear to everyone."

"Good for you—you completed the first milestone."

"You can send that video preview to the client when you finish it."

"Let's not tell Ben about this problem—it could blow our budget."

"I don't see why you think the video software is hard to use."

"We have so much more work to do—I hope no one has plans for this weekend."

Managing Meetings

Meetings are a regular part of organizational life, especially if you are a member of a team. Teams have meetings to collaborate and communicate. They also meet to solve problems, make decisions, and plan projects and other activities. If you are the team leader, the success of the meeting is up to you. If you are attending but not leading a meeting, you can help make meetings productive and worthwhile. In this unit, you will learn about the most common types of meetings. You will also learn how to plan, conduct, and conclude meetings. You have been working at the Chicago branch office of Quest Specialty Travel for about a year. Your manager, Don Novak, wants to build on your success with the training guide team, and asks you to participate in a new team. The goal of this team is to upgrade the Web site for the Chicago branch office. Don expects the team to meet frequently, so you want to develop your meeting management skills.

OBJECTIVES

Understand the role of meetings

Plan meetings

Develop meeting agendas

Schedule meetings

Conduct meetings effectively

Take notes and publish minutes

Conclude meetings and create
action plans

Solve common meeting problems

Understanding the Role of Meetings

Meetings are a staple in most organizations. Professional staff and managers typically attend a few meetings every week. Senior executives regularly spend over half their working hours in meetings and conferences. In its most basic form, a **meeting** is when three or more people get together at a common time to discuss, debate, decide, plan, and solve problems related to a company goal. Table E-1 summarizes when a team should hold a meeting and when it should send a written message, such as an e-mail, text message, or memo. Many meetings occur in a physical location where participants can talk face to face. Electronic communications also make it possible to have a virtual meeting with people who are in different places. See Figure E-1. In either case, meetings provide valuable contact with others and let you observe the verbal and nonverbal cues of other participants. You should be familiar with the most common types of meetings and the role they play in a team and an organization. To prepare for your new assignment to the Web site upgrade team, you want to review the basics of holding and attending team meetings.

DETAILS

Teams hold meetings for the following reasons:

- **Sharing information**

  Teams hold meetings to exchange information. Informational meetings provide opportunities to ask and answer questions, pool information, and make sure everyone hears and understands the same news. For example, you might hold an informational meeting to introduce a new team member, announce a team success, report on updates to a project, or provide limited training. Informational meetings can be called only when necessary or scheduled on a regular basis.

- **Solving problems**

  When a team faces a complicated problem, it might hold a meeting to discuss and resolve the problem. Team leaders might call a problem-solving meeting as soon as they learn about a problem. For this reason, they do not provide an agenda in advance or support information during the meeting. In some cases, the meeting is the first time that many participants learn about the problem. Usually, the team assesses the scope and impact of the problem, and then the group works to identify possible solutions.

- **Planning**

  Teams often use meetings to make plans. They organize and coordinate team activities and tasks. Unlike problem-solving meetings, team leaders should organize planning meetings in advance. They should distribute material to team members before the meeting so everyone is prepared to participate.

> **QUICK TIP**
> Update meetings are also called status meetings or department meetings.

- **Providing updates**

  Teams often use regularly scheduled meetings to keep all members up to date on the team's progress. Typically, a team meets at least once a week. The tone of these meetings is usually informal to encourage open communication. Some update meetings are **feedback meetings**, where participants have the chance to report their progress on assigned tasks. They can also discuss problems and ask for suggestions to solve the problems. Other update meetings are **feedforward meetings**, where participants look ahead, instead of looking toward the past. In feedforward meetings, teams discuss schedules for the immediate future and coordinate activities.

- **Making decisions**

  Teams occasionally need to meet so they can work cooperatively on a decision. Examples of these meetings include reviewing applications to hire an employee, setting goals for the next stage of a project, or evaluating bids from prospective contractors. In each case, the goal of the meeting is to make a decision.

FIGURE E-1: Virtual meeting

© Andresr, 2010

TABLE E-1: Determining whether to hold a meeting

scenario	hold meeting	send written message
Team members attended a conference on the latest Web technologies and now want to share what they learned	•	
You reviewed the Web sites of other travel companies and want to report on what you found	•	
A team member completed a preliminary outline of the new Web site and wants to ask for feedback	•	
Your manager announced a new Internet usage policy, and you want to discuss how it affects the team	•	
Some team members have selected two possible designs for the updated Web site and want to seek consensus from the entire team	•	
The software the team is using to create Web pages is too difficult, which is causing delays	•	
The team leader wants to invite members to attend a team meeting		•
You need to tell everyone on your team that a meeting is being postponed		•
Team members need to review the details of a plan		•
The team leader wants to remind everyone about due dates they agreed to meet		•

Planning Meetings

Effective meetings are a valuable use of the participants' time. Ineffective meetings are unproductive and frustrating. The difference between the two often comes down to the planning that preceded the meeting. To run an effective meeting, you need to plan who will attend and what you will discuss. Although the Web site upgrade team does not have a team leader yet, Don suggests you run the first team meeting. Before you do, you take time to plan the meeting.

1. Start with the objective

Although you might hold meetings for different reasons, they each have a major objective. Start by defining the purpose of the meeting. You should be able to express the purpose in a few words. Don't start planning the meeting until you have a clear idea of its goal.

2. Make sure you need a meeting

Some organizations prefer meetings to other types of communication and hold them frequently. Keep in mind that a meeting is expensive because it consumes the time of all the participants. If someone has to travel to participate in the meeting, it becomes even more costly. Sometimes you can accomplish your objective without having everyone get together. Could an e-mail message, online discussion, or memo meet your goals? If so, try to use them before calling a meeting.

> **QUICK TIP**
> Call attendees personally if you want to be sure they will attend.

3. Identify key participants

If you decide that a meeting is the best way to meet your goal, decide who should participate. Ask yourself who needs to attend to make the meeting successful. The purpose of the meeting often determines the number of people to invite. See Figure E-2. If some participants will present information or play an active role in the meeting, give them time to prepare. If others would directly benefit from attending, add them to your invitation list.

> **QUICK TIP**
> Add only appropriate items to the agenda.

4. Distribute an agenda and information in advance

At least 2 days before the meeting, send out an **agenda**, which is a list of topics that will be discussed during the meeting. See Figure E-3. Include other information such as reports that participants should read before the meeting. Never start a meeting by passing out materials such as copies of documents or presentation slides. These are distractions and disrupt your meeting. You want to give people enough time to get prepared and come to the meeting ready to work. You can also ask people what they want to discuss. Add these items to the agenda. Give people something to do so they become vested in the meeting and its outcome.

> **QUICK TIP**
> Try to locate the meeting close to as many people as you can—not somewhere that is only convenient for you.

5. Choose an appropriate setting

Select a time and place that is convenient for most of the attendees. Be sensitive to other obligations and scheduling conflicts as you select a meeting time.

1. Use a word processor such as Microsoft Office Word to open the file E-1.doc provided with your Data Files, and save it as Meeting Plan.doc in the location where you store your Data Files

2. Read the contents of Meeting Plan.doc, which describe the plans for a meeting

3. Complete the meeting agenda

4. Save and close Meeting Plan.doc, then submit it to your instructor as requested

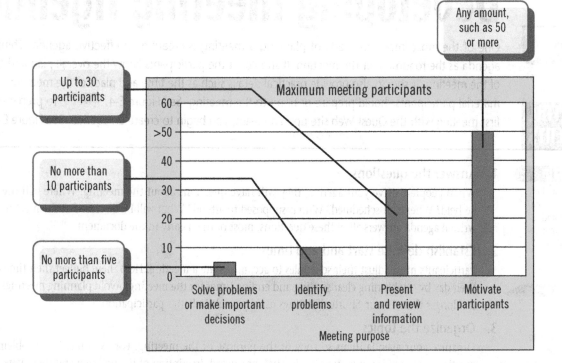

Maximum meeting participants

Meeting purpose: Solve problems or make important decisions · Identify problems · Present and review information · Motivate participants

Up to 30 participants

No more than 10 participants

No more than five participants

Any amount, such as 50 or more

FIGURE E-3: Outline for a meeting agenda

Agenda: Meeting Title

Date
Start and End Time
Location

I.   Call to Order
II.   Roll Call
III.   Approval of Last Meeting's Minutes
IV.   Chairperson's Report
        a.
        b.
V.   Committee Reports
        a.
        b.
VI.   Old Business
        a.
        b.
VII.   New Business
        a.
        b.
VIII.   Announcements
IX.   Adjournment

Developing Meeting Agendas

One of the most important parts of planning a meeting is creating an effective agenda. Think of the agenda as the roadmap for the meeting. It should let the participants know the overall plan and direction of the meeting. It should also provide practical details such as the time and place of the meeting and what material participants should prepare or bring to the meeting. See Figure E-4. To prepare for your first meeting with the Quest Web site upgrade team, you begin to create an agenda. See Figure E-5.

ESSENTIAL ELEMENTS

1. Answer the questions

When people receive your agenda, they will have questions about the meeting. Where will the meeting be held? When is it scheduled? Who is supposed to attend? What will be discussed at the meeting? A well-written agenda answers all of these questions, most of them early in the document.

QUICK TIP
Proofread a draft of your agenda before circulating it and make sure that it answers all of these questions.

2. Establish definite start and end times

Participants must adjust their schedules to accommodate a meeting. Help them budget their time and plan their day by establishing clear starting and ending times for the meeting. Avoid planning meetings that will last longer than 1 hour. Shorter meetings usually result in better participation.

QUICK TIP
If a meeting is scheduled for 90 minutes or longer, be sure to plan for a break.

3. Organize the topics

Organize your agenda items so they fit the purpose of the meeting. For example, in a problem-solving meeting, you could start with a simple, straightforward description of the problem and then work toward a lively discussion of possible solutions. This organization lets everyone adjust to the meeting dynamics and feel comfortable with the other participants before the hard work begins. You can also organize topics chronologically. For example, you might review the action items from an earlier meeting before moving on to new action items.

4. List estimated times for each agenda item

If the agenda includes several items, list how much time should be devoted to each item. These estimates let everyone know how long the discussion should last. Without the estimates, the team might dwell too long on a particular issue. Be realistic with your estimates and flexible during the meeting. Don't arbitrarily cut someone off because the time limit has run out.

QUICK TIP
Allow 1–2 days to review the agenda and provide feedback. If you make changes, send updated copies to everyone as soon as you can.

5. Circulate the meeting agenda in advance

Prepare your agenda in advance of the meeting, and circulate copies to the attendees. You can also send a copy to managers interested in the team or the meeting topic. Sending an agenda as an e-mail attachment is appropriate and often the fastest way to deliver the document.

YOU TRY IT

1. Use a word processor such as Microsoft Office Word to open the file E-2.doc provided with your Data Files, and save it as Meeting Agenda.doc in the location where you store your Data Files

2. Read the contents of Meeting Agenda.doc, which contain a partial agenda

3. Complete the meeting agenda

4. Save and close Meeting Agenda.doc, then submit it to your instructor as requested

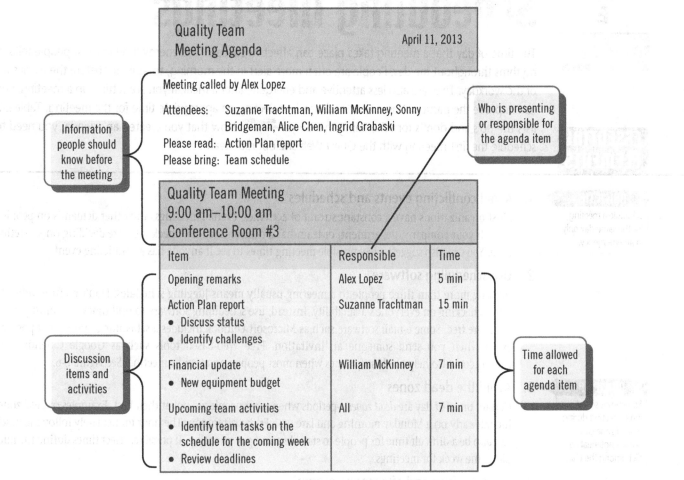

Quality Team
Meeting Agenda
April 11, 2013

Meeting called by Alex Lopez

Attendees: Suzanne Trachtman, William McKinney, Sonny
Bridgeman, Alice Chen, Ingrid Grabaski
Please read: Action Plan report
Please bring: Team schedule

Information people should know before the meeting

Who is presenting or responsible for the agenda item

Quality Team Meeting
9:00 am–10:00 am
Conference Room #3

Item	Responsible	Time
Opening remarks	Alex Lopez	5 min
Action Plan report • Discuss status • Identify challenges	Suzanne Trachtman	15 min
Financial update • New equipment budget	William McKinney	7 min
Upcoming team activities • Identify team tasks on the schedule for the coming week • Review deadlines	All	7 min

Discussion items and activities

Time allowed for each agenda item

FIGURE E-5: Meeting agenda for Quest Web site upgrade team

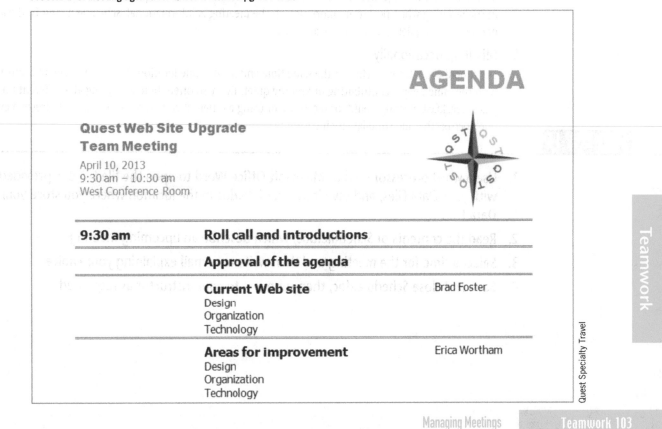

AGENDA

**Quest Web Site Upgrade
Team Meeting**

April 10, 2013
9:30 am – 10:30 am
West Conference Room

9:30 am	**Roll call and introductions**	
	Approval of the agenda	
	Current Web site Design Organization Technology	Brad Foster
	Areas for improvement Design Organization Technology	Erica Wortham

Quest Specialty Travel

Teamwork

Scheduling Meetings

UNIT E — Teamwork

ESSENTIAL ELEMENTS

The time of day that a meeting takes place can affect its success. The energy level of most people follows rhythms throughout the day. People are often more alert in the morning, though not before the usual start of the workday. They are also less attentive and energetic after a meal. If you are setting up a meeting, you can improve the participation and attendance by selecting an appropriate time for the meeting. Table E-2 lists the do's and don'ts for scheduling meetings. Now that you created an agenda, you need to schedule the first meeting with the Quest Web site upgrade team.

1. Avoid conflicting events and schedules

> **QUICK TIP**
> Schedule a meeting for the same day only in an emergency.

Most organizations have a constant stream of activities, events, meetings, and other demands on people's time. If your company, department, or team has a central calendar, check it before deciding on a meeting time. You can also suggest a few possible meeting times to see if anyone has a conflicting event.

2. Use scheduling software

Inviting more than three people to a meeting usually means juggling schedules. Don't go from office to office checking on everyone's availability. Instead, use scheduling software to find times that most participants are free. Some e-mail software such as Microsoft Outlook includes a scheduling option that posts an event when you send someone an invitation. Free Web-based tools such as Google Calendar and Doodle.com also help to identify times when most people can attend a meeting. See Figure E-6.

3. Avoid the dead zones

> **QUICK TIP**
> Sometimes scheduling a meeting during a dead zone can reduce potential conflict among the team.

Certain times of day are *dead zones*—periods when most people are not at their best. Examples of dead zones include early on a Monday morning and late on a Friday afternoon. The hour immediately following lunch can also be a difficult time for people to stay alert and pay attention. If possible, select times during the middle of the week for meetings.

4. Use mornings and afternoons properly

Your energy level and alertness change throughout the day. You can take advantage of this when you schedule meetings. If the objective of the meeting involves creative activity or problem solving, select a start time in the morning when people are more alert. If the meeting is informational, schedule it later in the afternoon to have a quieter, more passive audience.

5. Mix it up occasionally

Don't hold every team meeting at the same time and in the same location. Teams can easily fall into a rut, with the same people contributing or keeping quiet. Every so often, hold a meeting at a different time or place. Breakfast meetings, outdoor meetings, or using a different conference room can help freshen everyone's perspective and stimulate their creativity.

YOU TRY IT

1. Use a word processor such as Microsoft Office Word to open the file E-3.doc provided with your Data Files, and save it as Schedule.doc in the location where you store your Data Files

2. Read the contents of Schedule.doc, which describe an upcoming meeting

3. Select a time for the meeting and then write an e-mail explaining your choice

4. Save and close Schedule.doc, then submit it to your instructor as requested

FIGURE E-6: Using scheduling software to find a suitable meeting time

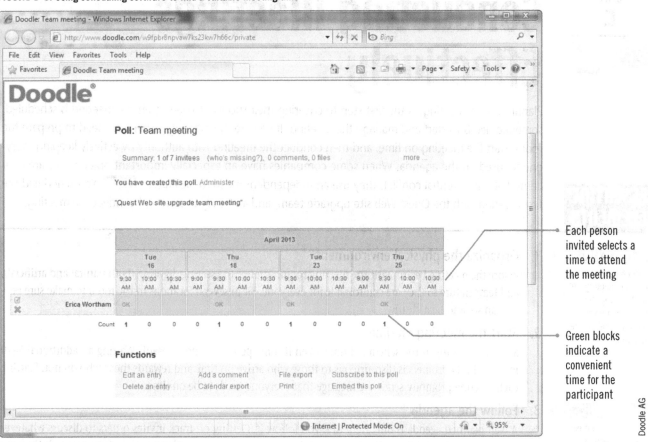

Each person invited selects a time to attend the meeting

Green blocks indicate a convenient time for the participant

Doodle AG

TABLE E-2: Scheduling meetings do's and don'ts

guideline	do	don't
Avoid conflicts	• Check a central calendar for upcoming events • Suggest possible meeting times and ask participants to identify which time are busy for them • Use scheduling software to automate inviting people and scheduling meetings	• **Don't** physically check with each participant to see when he or she can meet • **Don't** postpone a meeting if everyone cannot attend; select a time that works for most people
Consider the time of day	• Recognize that very early in the morning, late in the afternoon, and right after a meal are difficult times for meetings • Schedule active meetings in the morning • Schedule informational meetings for the afternoon	• **Don't** schedule a meeting during a dead zone, such as early Monday morning • **Don't** start a meeting that requires active participation at a time most people have low energy levels
Mix it up	• Occasionally hold a meeting at a different time or place, such as outdoors	• **Don't** hold all team meetings at the same time and place

Online meeting schedulers

The more people invited to a meeting, the more difficult it is to find a time convenient for everyone. Sending out e-mails asking people for their preferred times can take many rounds of time-consuming messages. A better solution is to use a Web service to schedule meetings. This category of software lets you select dates and times on a calendar, and then invite your colleagues to choose the ones that work for them. You view the responses to find a time that's best for most people. Besides Google Calendar and Doodle.com (mentioned earlier in this lesson), you can use Timebridge. TimeBridge (*http://timebridge.com*) lets you use your electronic calendar as you schedule. Its notable feature is how easily participants can respond. TimeBridge asks the people you invite to select Yes, No, or Best for each time you suggest. If a time is best for all participants, TimeBridge sets that as the time for the meeting.

Conducting Meetings Effectively

Planning team meetings is the first step to ensuring their success. However, after a meeting is scheduled, someone needs to start and manage the meeting. If you are the meeting leader, you need to prepare the room, start the meeting on time, and then conduct the meeting with authority by actively keeping everyone focused on the agenda. When some companies have an especially important objective or are concerned about potential conflict, they use an independent meeting facilitator. You scheduled the first meeting with the Quest Web site upgrade team, and are ready to start and conduct the meeting.

ESSENTIAL ELEMENTS

QUICK TIP

If you are organizing a virtual meeting, set up the computer and software you need well before the meeting.

1. **Organize the physical environment**

   Before the meeting begins, visit the meeting room. Arrange the seating, lighting (both natural and artificial), and temperature so they are comfortable for everyone. Sit in several locations in the room to make sure people can see and hear clearly.

2. **Start the meeting on time**

   Start the meeting at the scheduled time, even if some people are not present. Waiting an additional 5–10 minutes for latecomers is discourteous to those who arrive on time and rewards those who do not. Starting each meeting promptly sends the message that everyone needs to be on time.

QUICK TIP

After starting a meeting, the meeting leader's job is to say little while keeping everyone on track.

3. **Follow the agenda**

   A well-planned agenda is only helpful if you follow it. Getting off track invites others to discuss whatever seems appropriate to them. Keep a copy of the agenda in plain view along with a clock or watch that you can refer to. Occasionally call attention to the time, and move the meeting along in a courteous but businesslike manner. If you are not leading a meeting, you can participate actively by following the suggestions in Table E-3.

4. **Use a variety of presentation methods**

   To keep people's attention and encourage their participation, schedule more than one speaker and presentation method. Don't let someone lecture or display a slideshow for the length of the meeting. Change the tone or format every 10–15 minutes to stimulate interest. Figure E-7 shows part of an agenda that lists a variety of presentation methods.

5. **Postpone lengthy discussion items**

   Some meeting topics trigger long discussions or digressions. Unless you sense that getting sidetracked is leading to a uniquely creative or motivating moment, postpone lengthy debates until the end of the meeting. Keep a list of topics to cover in another meeting.

QUICK TIP

Use e-mail to share informational items or to allow people to vote on minor matters.

6. **Finish on time**

   Just as you start on time, you should also finish on time. Allowing a meeting to run late is disrespectful of your attendees' time and schedules. If the team cannot cover all the agenda items in the scheduled time, move them to the next meeting.

YOU TRY IT

1. Use a word processor such as Microsoft Office Word to open the file E-4.doc provided with your Data Files, and save it as Conduct.doc in the location where you store your Data Files

2. Read the contents of Conduct.doc, which describe a meeting

3. Evaluate the pros and cons of the meeting

4. Save and close Conduct.doc, then submit it to your instructor as requested

FIGURE E-7: Meeting with a variety of presentation methods

9:30 am	Roll call and introductions		5 min
	Meeting ground rules	Louisa Greene	10 min discussion
	Current Web site Design Organization Technology	Brad Foster	10 min slide show
	Areas for improvement Design Organization Technology	Erica Wortham	15 min brainstorming
	Practical considerations Files and other resources Contractors Schedule	John Hassen and Don Novak	10 min handouts

Discussion, slide show, brainstorming, and handouts create variety

TABLE E-3: Participating in meetings effectively

suggestions	actions
Prepare for the meeting	• Collect requested materials, such as notes and reports • Read the agenda • Prepare notes, questions, and comments about the agenda items
Arrive early	• Arrive at the meeting room a few minutes before the scheduled time • Make sure you have the materials and supplies you need • Serve yourself any refreshments and then take your seat
Contribute constructively	• Phrase your comments so they are positive and constructive—offer solutions or alternatives with your criticisms • Use a neutral, energetic tone of voice • Comment on ideas and tasks, not on other people • Give credit to your teammates • Express your views to everyone during the meeting, not afterwards or only to one or two other people
Use common courtesy	• Wait for your turn to speak—don't interrupt others • Thank the meeting leader and the participants for their contributions • Turn off your cell phone and leave your computer at your desk

Taking Notes and Publishing Minutes

To help establish a shared record of what the team discussed and decided during a meeting, someone should take notes. Afterwards, distill those notes into meeting **minutes**, which serve as an official written record of the meeting. Minutes usually follow the format shown in Figure E-8. Team members can refer to the minutes to clear up misunderstandings or disagreements. If someone did not attend the meeting, they can use the minutes to learn about the discussion and decisions the team made. Table E-4 lists the do's and don'ts for taking notes and publishing minutes. At the meeting of the Quest Web site upgrade team, John Hassen offers to take notes and produce the minutes. You review the basics of notes and minutes before he starts.

ESSENTIAL ELEMENTS

QUICK TIP
The note taker can stand at a flip chart or whiteboard to take notes that everyone can see.

1. Assign a note taker in advance

Don't start a meeting by asking people to volunteer for roles such as note taker. Doing so scatters attention instead of focusing it. Instead, ask someone before the meeting to take notes and prepare the minutes. To avoid taking advantage of one team member, rotate the note-taking task. Select an order, such as alphabetical by last name, at the first team meeting.

2. Don't do double duty

The meeting leader seems like the most natural person to take notes and draft the meeting minutes. Unfortunately, this seldom works well in practice. If you are leading the meeting, you have to pay attention to the proceedings and make certain that everyone is involved and participating. Taking notes involves observing and clarifying, so you can't play both roles.

QUICK TIP
Use a generic meeting minutes template to simplify the process for your note taker.

3. Keep the broader audience in mind

Meeting minutes provide a summary of what went on during the meeting. They are a useful reminder for those who attended. Others also read and reference the minutes, so make sure your minutes are fit for a broad audience. Don't include confidential, sensitive, or embarrassing information. Use positive language and keep the contents objective.

QUICK TIP
Formal meetings or legal hearings do often record every speaker's words verbatim.

4. Capture key decisions and discussion items

If you are taking notes for a team meeting, you don't need to write down what everyone says and does precisely. Summarize the important decisions and discussion items. Include people's names when appropriate, but don't include verbatim dialogue, disagreements, or references to conflict.

5. Distribute minutes promptly

Organize the meeting notes and compile them into a formal set of meeting minutes as soon as possible. Ideally, distribute the minutes of a meeting within 24 hours. Send a copy to all of the participants as an e-mail attachment and ask them to review it for accuracy and completeness. Include a way for people to make corrections, suggest changes, and provide general feedback. At your next team meeting, ask the group to endorse or accept these minutes as edited.

YOU TRY IT

1. Use a word processor such as Microsoft Office Word to open the file E-5.doc provided with your Data Files, and save it as Minutes.doc in the location where you store your Data Files

2. Read the contents of Minutes.doc, which include meeting notes

3. Write the minutes of this meeting

4. Save and close Minutes.doc, then submit it to your instructor as requested

Quest Web Site Upgrade
Team Meeting

April 10, 2013
9:30 am – 10:30 am
West Conference Room

Meeting leader:	Louisa Greene	Recorder:	John Hassen
Present:	Brad Foster, Louisa Greene, John Hassen, Gary Mitchell, Don Novak, Erica Wortham	**Absent:**	Patty DeCheine

Information about who attended the meeting

Minutes

Agenda item:	Meeting ground rules	Presenter:	Louisa Greene
Discussion:	Set the ground rules for team meetings		
Conclusions:	The team will arrive to meetings on time, communicate openly, support team members, listen carefully, participate fully, confront conflict directly, and follow the agenda.		

Summarizes the first agenda item

Action items		Person responsible	Deadline
✓ Print meeting ground rules		John Hassen	4/14/13

First action item

Quest Specialty Travel

TABLE E-4: Taking notes and publishing minutes do's and don'ts

guideline	do	don't
Assign a note taker	• Ask someone before the meeting to take notes and prepare the minutes • Rotate the recording task	• **Don't** start a meeting asking for volunteers to take notes and write the minutes • **Don't** accept the role of note taker if you are also the meeting leader
Record decisions and summarize the discussion	• Summarize the main events of the meeting • Write the minutes for two audiences: meeting attendees and others in the organization • Use positive or neutral language in the minutes	• **Don't** include confidential, sensitive, or embarrassing information in the minutes • **Don't** record what everyone says exactly unless you have a legal requirement to do so
Publish minutes	• Distribute the minutes within 24 hours of the meeting, if possible • Send a copy of the minutes to all participants • Ask participants to review the minutes for accuracy and completeness	**Don't** distribute minutes without providing a way for people to offer feedback

Rules of order

Many formal groups, including corporate boards, legislatures, clubs, and committees, follow standard rules of order. These rules are also called **parliamentary procedure**, which set how the group discusses topics and makes decisions during meetings. Most of the rules address how to debate questions and reach group decisions fairly, usually by vote. For example, one basic principle of parliamentary procedure is that a group can debate only one subject at a time. Another principle is that each member of

the group has rights that are equal to every other member. In the United States, the most common set of rules are *Robert's Rules of Order*. According to Rachel Donadio in the *New York Times*, this instruction manual "presents a clear, if highly technical, vision of how democracy works."

Source: Donadio, Rachel, "Point of Order," *New York Times*, May 20, 2007.

Teamwork

Concluding Meetings and Creating Action Plans

Effective meetings should come to a clear and logical ending. All participants should know what was resolved and what they are responsible for. They should be able to describe the decisions the team made and the actions they took. Conclude a meeting by indicating it is time to end, summarizing the key issues and decisions made, and then creating an action plan. An **action plan** is a list of tasks to perform and assignments showing who is responsible for their completion. See Figure E-9. Table E-5 lists the do's and don'ts for concluding meetings. You are reaching the end of your agenda during the meeting of the Quest Web site upgrade team. You are ready to conclude the meeting and create an action plan.

1. Summarize the discussion and decisions

During the meeting, make quick notes of topics you want to revisit. At the end of the meeting, you can refer to these notes to summarize what the team agreed to do. Your notes can be the basis for the action plan.

2. Identify specific actions

Start an action plan by listing the specific details of your next tasks. Don't make the mistake of merely summarizing the steps. Identify what the expected outcome should look like. For example, instead of saying, "We need to wrap up the Web site proposal pretty soon," you should say, "The team should create a 10-page proposal with price quotes and deliver it to Don Novak by May 1."

3. Assign responsibility

Break down the tasks so you can assign a task to a single person. If a group of people is collectively responsible, they can easily assume someone else is taking care of the task. A group can work together, but one person should be responsible for each task the group completes. Be clear and specific with these assignments, as in, "Patty, please hand-deliver the completed Web site proposal to Don by May 1."

4. Set deadlines

The priority people assign to a task is usually based on when it must be completed. Without a clear deadline, assignments are often overlooked in favor of more pressing matters. Assign a due date or time to every item in your action plan.

5. Follow up

Determine how the team leader will follow up on assignments. Should each person send an e-mail message to the group to report on their progress? Should everyone update the team at the next meeting? Also follow up on ideas, topics, and agenda items you could not cover during the meeting by adding them to the agenda for a later meeting.

1. Use a word processor such as Microsoft Office Word to open the file E-6.doc provided with your Data Files, and save it as Actions.doc in the location where you store your Data Files

2. Read the contents of Actions.doc, which include meeting notes

3. Based on the notes, complete the action plan in the document

4. Save and close Actions.doc, then submit it to your instructor as requested

Quest Web Site Upgrade
Action Plan

April 10, 2013

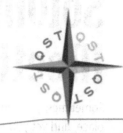

Who is responsible

Actions	Assigned to	Due Date	Resources
Step 1: Make copies of files for current Web site and store on main office computer	John Hassen	4/17/13	Needs to access company backups
Step 2: Find resource for graphics: list contact information and prices	Erica Wortham	4/17/13	$500 budget available
Step 3: Review at least five Web sites for similar companies	Brad Foster Louisa Greene	4/17/13	4 hours each
Step 4: Create a 10-15 minute presentation on Web sites reviewed	Brad Foster Louisa Greene	4/24/13	4 hours each

Specific steps

Due dates

What each person needs to complete the task

Quest Specialty Travel

TABLE E-5: Concluding meetings and creating action plans do's and don'ts

guideline	do	don't
Conclude the meeting	• During the meeting, note which topics you want to revisit when you conclude • Summarize the discussion and decisions • Start the action plan by listing specific details of the next tasks • Describe the expected outcome	**Don't** summarize the steps in the action plan; be specific
Assign responsibility	• Make sure one person is responsible for completing a task • Clearly state the details of the assignment, answering the who, what, where, when, and how questions • Set a deadline for completing each task	• **Don't** assign a task to the group as a whole • **Don't** assign a task without including a due date
Follow up	• Make sure everyone knows how to follow up on assignments • Identify ideas, topics, and agenda items to add to the agenda for a later meeting	**Don't** assign a task without letting the person know how to deliver the results

Teamwork

Solving Common Meeting Problems

Sometimes, you can carefully plan a meeting, draft and organize your agenda, choose an ideal time and place, and yet you still run into difficulties. Keep in mind that meetings are designed for human interaction and conflicts are natural in this setting. Conflict often develops if people feel their views are not being heard or understood. Respond to conflict and other problems in a calm, rational manner. Those in attendance will take their cues from you and respond accordingly. You can also prepare for conflict by understanding common meeting problems and how to deal with them. Table E-6 outlines the do's and don'ts for solving common meeting problems. Before you plan the next meeting of the Quest Web site upgrade team, Don Novak suggests you learn how to confront common meeting problems.

1. Balance participation

During a meeting, everyone should have a chance to share their views. However, one or more meeting participants can dominate the discussion, especially during early meetings when others are still reserved. If someone is long-winded during a meeting that you are leading, be sure to deal with them politely, but directly. Use physical gestures such as raising your hand to catch their attention and create a pause in their talking. Figure E-10 shows other ways to balance participation.

2. Involve the wallflowers

Everyone at a meeting should participate actively and feel they can share their views with the team. Invite reserved or quiet team members to speak up by asking questions. For example, you could say, "Gary, what do you think about the sample Web page?" Be sensitive to a shy team member's response. Don't press them if they are reluctant to participate.

3. Handle disputes

Team members have disputes even on the most cohesive teams. If a conflict develops during a team meeting, try to cool it off before the situation boils over. Let each person state their case while everyone is listening. Often, airing an opinion or making a statement reduces anger and frustration. Don't take sides, but summarize what they said, and let the group offer comments. If the team members remain tense, take a brief break or save the discussion for another meeting.

4. Deal with tardiness and absence

How should you deal with the team member who shows up late to a meeting or skips it altogether? As a rule, don't delay a meeting unless you need to wait for a guest. When someone does arrive late, don't call attention to them or review what the team covered. Continue with the agenda. Check up on absent team members later. Knowing that you valued their attendance enough to follow up usually motivates them to attend the next meeting.

1. Use a word processor such as Microsoft Office Word to open the file E-7.doc provided with your Data Files, and save it as Meeting Problems.doc in the location where you store your Data Files

2. Read the contents of Meeting Problems.doc, which describe a meeting

3. Identify how to solve the problems in the meeting

4. Save and close Meeting Problems.doc, then submit it to your instructor as requested

FIGURE E-10: Balancing participation in a meeting

Problem: Erica has strong opinions and is not letting other people speak

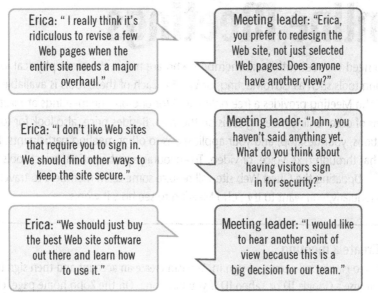

Erica: "I really think it's ridiculous to revise a few Web pages when the entire site needs a major overhaul."

Meeting leader: "Erica, you prefer to redesign the Web site, not just selected Web pages. Does anyone have another view?"

Erica: "I don't like Web sites that require you to sign in. We should find other ways to keep the site secure."

Meeting leader: "John, you haven't said anything yet. What do you think about having visitors sign in for security?"

Erica: "We should just buy the best Web site software out there and learn how to use it."

Meeting leader: "I would like to hear another point of view because this is a big decision for our team."

TABLE E-6: Solving common meeting problems do's and don'ts

guideline	do	don't
Balance participation	• Encourage each person at a meeting to speak • Gently discourage people from dominating the meeting • Catch the attention of a long-winded participant so you can say something like "We'll have to talk about that later because we need to return to the topic of . . ." • Invite quieter or reserved team members to speak • Ask questions to encourage everyone to participate	• **Don't** allow someone to introduce new discussion topics or to digress; say something like "We are getting off track, so let's return to the current topic" • **Don't** force a quiet or shy person to speak if they are reluctant to do so
Handle conflict	• Deal with a dispute immediately and directly • Let each person state their views • Ask team members to comment or offer suggestions • Take a break if necessary to reduce tension	• **Don't** ignore the conflict or let the awkwardness it causes linger • **Don't** take sides
Respond to tardiness and absence	• Continue with the agenda • Check up on absent team members to find out why they missed the meeting	• **Don't** delay a meeting while you wait for a participant • **Don't** make sarcastic comments about a team member's tardiness or try to embarrass them

Technology @ Work: Online Meetings

If you need to meet with team members who are not in the same physical location, you can use online meeting tools such as GoToMeeting, or WebEx. Each of these tools is available for a monthly subscription fee. Zoho Meeting provides a free online tool for one-on-one meetings at *meeting.zoho.com*. You can find dozens of other online meeting tools on the Web. Besides price, also look for tools that let you display presentations, your desktop, and your applications to other meeting participants. Most meeting software lets you chat through text, voice, or video. To encourage participation, select tools that run in a Web browser. Updating the Quest Web site will require some team members to travel. To continue meeting with them regularly, you want to try Zoho Meeting to see how it works.

ESSENTIAL ELEMENTS

1. Create a meeting

Go to *meeting.zoho.com* and sign in. You can create an account and then sign in with your Zoho ID, or you can use a Google ID or Yahoo ID if you have one. On the Zoho home page, click the Create Meeting button. A Web page opens where you can enter meeting information. See Figure E-11. Click the Create button to create a meeting and receive a meeting ID.

2. Invite participants

Using the free one-on-one meeting tool, you can invite one other person to the meeting through Zoho. You can invite many other people by sending them an e-mail message that tells them to go to *http://zohom.com*, click Join, and then enter the meeting ID. You can also send a link in the e-mail message that participants can click to go directly to the meeting page.

3. Start the meeting

When you set up the meeting, Zoho Meeting sends you an e-mail invitation along with your participants. To start the meeting, open the e-mail message, and then click Start Meeting. Review the meeting details, and then click the Start button. Zoho installs some software for you, and then displays meeting tools. See Figure E-12.

Everything you display on your desktop is also displayed to your participants. You can communicate with each other by typing chat messages or by using the phone. When you're finished, close the Web browser to end the meeting.

YOU TRY IT

1. **Open a Web browser such as Microsoft Internet Explorer or Mozilla Firefox, and go to** meeting.zoho.com

2. **Log on or create a free account at the site, if necessary**

3. **Click the Create Meeting button, enter information about a meeting to discuss a memorable trip with one of your classmates, and then click the Create button**

4. **Use e-mail to invite your classmate to join the meeting**

5. **When you receive an e-mail message about the meeting, click Create Meeting**

6. **Tell your classmate to join the meeting**

7. **Press the Print Screen key to take a screen shot of the meeting page, open a word-processing program such as Microsoft Office Word, press Ctrl+V to paste each screen shot in a new document, then send the document to your instructor**

FIGURE E-11: Creating a meeting at Zoho Meeting

Enter a meeting topic

Select a date and time

Enter an e-mail address of a participant

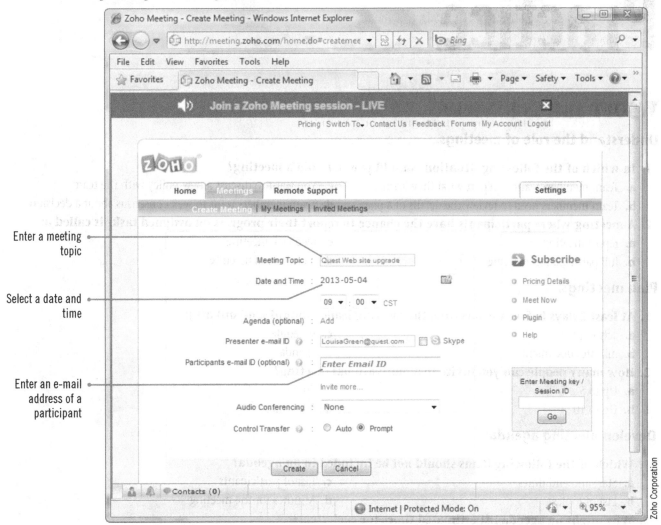

FIGURE E-12: Zoho meeting in progress

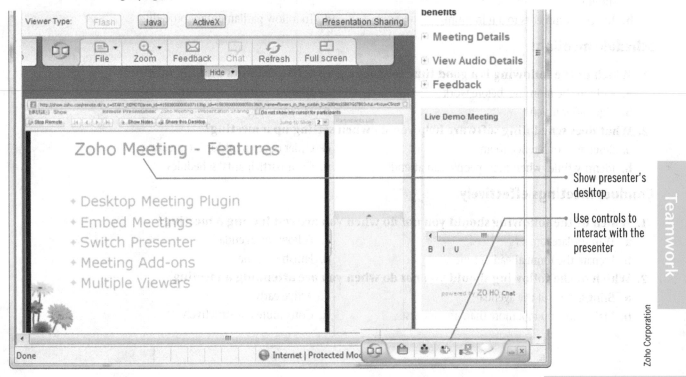

Show presenter's desktop

Use controls to interact with the presenter

Teamwork

Practice

▼ SOFT SKILLS REVIEW

Understand the role of meetings.

1. In which of the following situations should you *not* hold a meeting?
   a. Team members want to report what they learned
   b. Team members need to review the details of a plan
   c. You want to discuss a new policy with the team
   d. Team members want to seek consensus about a decision

2. A meeting where participants have the chance to report their progress on assigned tasks is called a:
   a. report meeting
   b. full participation meeting
   c. feedback meeting
   d. feedforward meeting

Plan meetings.

1. At least 2 days before the meeting, the meeting leader should send out a(n):
   a. action plan
   b. minutes document
   c. schedule
   d. agenda

2. How many people can you invite to a motivational meeting?
   a. Up to 5
   b. Up to 10
   c. 30
   d. 50 or more

Develop meeting agendas.

1. Which of the following items should *not* be included in an agenda?
   a. Start and end times
   b. List of topics
   c. List of participants
   d. Minutes for the meeting

2. Why might an agenda list estimated times for each item?
   a. To let everyone know how long the discussion should last
   b. To keep comments to a minimum
   c. To provide a reason to cut off a long-winded participant
   d. To follow parliamentary procedure

Schedule meetings.

1. Which of the following is a good time to schedule an active decision-making meeting?
   a. Early in the morning, before work
   b. Right after lunch
   c. Late on a Friday afternoon
   d. Midmorning

2. What does scheduling software help you do when setting up a meeting?
   a. Reserve a conference room
   b. Identify times when most people can attend
   c. Order equipment for the meeting
   d. Clear participants' schedules

Conduct meetings effectively.

1. Which of the following should you *not* do when you are conducting a meeting?
   a. Wait for latecomers
   b. Prepare the room ahead of time
   c. Follow the agenda
   d. Finish on time

2. Which of the following should you *not* do when you are attending a meeting?
   a. Bring a copy of the agenda
   b. Make sure you talk more than anyone else
   c. Arrive early
   d. Contribute constructively

Take notes and publish minutes.

1. **Meeting minutes are:**
   - **a.** the list of times allowed for each agenda item
   - **b.** times when all participants can attend
   - **c.** the official written record of the meeting
   - **d.** the time you cannot spend on other tasks

2. **What should you do to make sure notes are taken at team meetings?**
   - **a.** Start meetings by asking someone to volunteer to be the note taker
   - **b.** Rotate the note-taking task
   - **c.** Take the notes yourself
   - **d.** Create the notes after the meeting

Conclude meetings and create action plans.

1. **An action plan is:**
   - **a.** a summary of the decisions made at a meeting
   - **b.** a list of presentation methods
   - **c.** a detailed schedule
   - **d.** a list of tasks and assignments

2. **Which of the following should you *not* include in an action plan?**
   - **a.** Obstacles for completing a task
   - **b.** Who is responsible for each task
   - **c.** When the task is due
   - **d.** Detailed steps for completing the task

Solve common meeting problems.

1. **Which of the following is *not* a way to balance participation?**
   - **a.** Ask questions of quiet participants
   - **b.** Encourage each person to speak
   - **c.** Catch the attention of a long-winded participant
   - **d.** Allow someone to digress if the topic they introduce seems interesting

2. **What is an effective way to deal with a team member who shows up late to a meeting?**
   - **a.** Continue with the agenda
   - **b.** Delay the meeting until the team member arrives
   - **c.** Review what the team already covered
   - **d.** Call attention to the late team member

Technology @ Work: Online meeting tools

1. **When evaluating online meeting tools, what features should you look for?**
   - **a.** Ability to display your desktop to others
   - **b.** Ability to run in a Web browser
   - **c.** Ability to chat with participants
   - **d.** All of the above

2. **In Zoho Meeting, how can you invite people to an online meeting?**
   - **a.** Send an e-mail message
   - **b.** Post an invitation on their calendars
   - **c.** Start the meeting, and then call participants
   - **d.** Use special invitation software

▼ CRITICAL THINKING QUESTIONS

1. **Most people dislike meetings. However, professionals spend from 1–8 hours per week in meetings. What key factors might contribute to a person's dislike for meetings? How would you address this as a team member? As a team leader?**

2. **This unit mentions online meeting tools as a way to conduct a virtual meeting. What other types of tools can you use when participants cannot meet face to face? Do any of these tools provide advantages over physical meetings? If so, what are the advantages?**

3. **Consider the best and worst meetings you have attended. What characterized the best meetings? What characterized the worst? Be specific.**

4. **Many companies have employees in locations around the globe. Suppose you are conducting a meeting that involves people in five locations representing three cultures. Describe how you would prepare for such a meeting.**

5. You are conducting a meeting of your seven-member team. You sent everyone an agenda 2 days ago via e-mail, and you start the meeting on time by addressing the first item on the agenda. A few minutes later, when you are discussing the third agenda item, Roy bursts into the meeting room, pours himself a cup of coffee, and then sits down, placing his laptop computer and cell phone on the table. As another team member speaks, Roy says, "Hey, sorry to interrupt you, but I just lost track of time. What did I miss?" What do you do?

▼ INDEPENDENT CHALLENGE 1

You are the leader of the Customer Service team at Newberry Heating & Cooling, a contracting company in Columbus, Ohio. Your manager, Joanne Burton, asked your team to produce a guide for Customer Service employees. As you prepare for your first team meeting, Joanne gives you the agenda template shown in Figure E-13, and asks you to complete it and then distribute it to her and the meeting participants.

FIGURE E-13

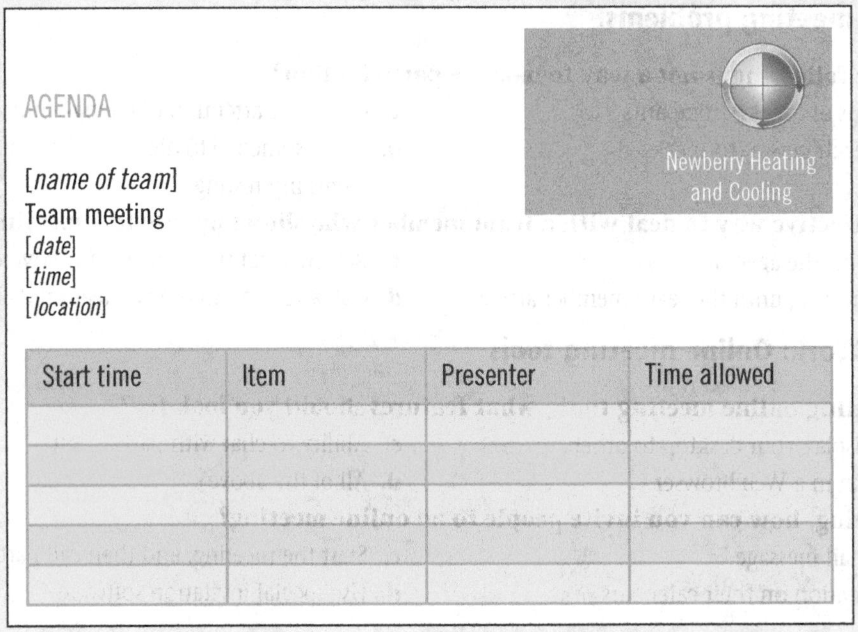

AGENDA

[name of team]
Team meeting
[date]
[time]
[location]

Newberry Heating
and Cooling

Start time	Item	Presenter	Time allowed

a. Use word-processing software such as Microsoft Office Word to open the file E-8.doc provided with your Data Files, and save it as Newberry Agenda.doc in the location where you store your Data Files.
b. Review the contents of Newberry Agenda.doc, which describe the upcoming Customer Service team meeting.
c. Complete the agenda in Newberry Agenda.doc based on the description of the meeting.
d. Submit the files to your instructor as requested.

▼ INDEPENDENT CHALLENGE 2

You work with George Lambert at a company called PT at Home, which provides physical therapy services to people in their homes. You have already successfully led a team at the company, and now George asks you to organize a new team. This team is responsible for finding ways to improve employee morale. After the first team meeting, you need to prepare an action plan. George gives you the template shown in Figure E-14.

FIGURE E-14

PT at Home

[team name]
Action Plan
[date]

Actions	Assigned to	Due Date	Resources
Step 1:			
Step 2:			
Step 3:			
Step 4:			

a. Use word-processing software such as Microsoft Office Word to open the file **E-9.doc** provided with your Data Files, and save it as **PT Action Plan.doc** in the location where you store your Data Files.

b. Read the description of the PT at Home Employee Morale team project, and then create the action plan in PT Action Plan.doc.

c. Submit the document to your instructor as requested.

▼ REAL LIFE INDEPENDENT CHALLENGE

The Wall Street Journal says that "the inability to run effective meetings can torpedo a career." To gain practice running meetings, complete the following activities:

a. Volunteer to lead a meeting for a group you belong to. The group might be a club, class, neighborhood organization, or sports team.

b. Define the purpose of the meeting.

c. Select and invite the participants, if necessary.

d. Create a meeting agenda that includes a statement of the meeting's purpose. List the participants. Include all the practical information you need, such as date and place of the meeting, the start and end time, and anything participants should prepare or bring to the meeting. List the topics you plan to cover and who will present them.

e. Distribute the agenda at least 2 days in advance of the meeting. Ask one participants to take notes and prepare minutes.

f. On the day of the meeting, prepare the meeting location. Start the meeting on time. If you think it's necessary, establish ground rules for the meeting, such as raising your hand to speak, letting each person speak, and contributing courteously.

g. Move the meeting along, encouraging everyone to participate. Try to avoid letting anyone dominate the meeting or digress from the agenda items. Summarize decisions and discussions along the way.

h. At the end of the meeting, review decisions and discuss action items.

i. Distribute the minutes a day or two after the meeting.

▼ TEAM CHALLENGE

You are working for Liz Montoya at Peachtree Landscapers, a landscaping company in Atlanta, Georgia. Liz is concerned that some employees are spending company time online visiting social networking sites and exchanging personal e-mail. She holds a company meeting to discuss the problem.

a. Working as a group, select a meeting leader. Assign half of the group members to take the point of view of banning the personal use of company computers completely. Assign the other half to take the point of view that Internet use should be restricted but not banned.

b. The meeting leader should start the meeting but not participate in the debate except to direct group members.

c. For at least 15 minutes, discuss the pros and cons of whether Peachtree Landscapers should ban the personal use of company computers or restrict Internet use.

d. After 15 minutes, discuss the most effective and least effective parts of the meeting.

▼ BE THE CRITIC

You are working for Viva Italia, an Italian restaurant with three locations in Chapel Hill, North Carolina. Alice Montgomery is going to hold a meeting with a small team to discuss ideas for new menu offerings. Alice performs the actions shown in Figure E-15. Review Alice's actions, and then identify those that do not help her manage effective meetings.

FIGURE E-15

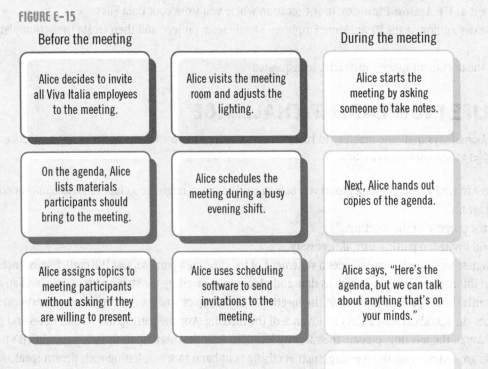

Glossary

Action plan A plan that summarizes the activities the group and other members of the organization agree to perform to make sure the project succeeds.

Ad hoc To have one specific purpose.

Challenge course Outdoor activities patterned after military obstacle courses that require the entire team's cooperation to help each participant overcome barriers. Also called a **ropes course.**

Change agent A person that can inspire or encourage others to change.

Cohesive team A team that works closely together, in which team members feel connected to other members.

Colleague A person that holds the same type of job as you do and usually works in the same company; a coworker. Also a co-worker united with you in common purpose.

Committee A group of people that discusses topics of interest to the whole organization.

Deliberative group A group or team that discusses or debates a topic, such as a committee that creates company policies.

Distributed team A team with members in different geographic locations.

Ego Part of the human psyche that governs a person's self-esteem.

Empower To enable others to think, behave, act, and make decisions with independence.

Equity Fairness, especially when applying rules.

Esprit de corps A quality that describes the increased motivation and morale that develops when people depend on each other.

Feedback meeting A meeting where participants have the chance to report their progress on assigned tasks.

Feedforward meeting A meeting where participants look ahead instead of to the past by discussing schedules for the immediate future and coordinating activities.

Functional decomposition Breaking down a complex system or set of processes into smaller parts, such as tasks.

Group Two or more people who interact with each other, share expectations and obligations, and develop a common identity as a group.

Group dynamics The way that people work and interact with each other.

Groupthink When groups become so cohesive that the members minimize conflict and support consensus without critically considering the merits of ideas and decisions.

High-performing team A team with people who develop chemistry with each other and work together very effectively.

Identity For a team, the set of qualities that makes others see the group as a whole and distinguishes the team from other similar groups.

Interdependencies Tasks that need to be completed before another task can begin.

Knowledge gap The difference in knowledge that appears when one person or group has access to information that another person or group does not.

Liaison A person who relays information between groups.

Logo A graphic that represents a company or other group.

Managing up Working with your direct supervisor and other managers in the company.

Meeting An activity that involves three or more people gathering to exchange information, make decisions, and solve problems.

Minutes An official written record of a meeting.

Norms The rules a group or team uses for appropriate and inappropriate values, beliefs, attitudes, and behaviors.

Organizational memory The history and culture that a group must function in, including the various processes, personalities, and subtleties of how the organization operates.

Parliamentary procedure Standard rules of order that set how a group discusses topics and makes decisions during meetings.

Project An activity with well-defined objectives or outcomes, a limited budget, and a schedule for completion.

Project closeout report A formal document that officially concludes a team project and releases team members from the assignment.

Proxy In a team, a coordinator who regularly contacts everyone, develops and manages the team's calendar, distributes information, and collects needed information and reports.

Quality circle A group of workers who identify and solve work-related problems.

Specialist In a team, a person with particular talents or abilities that are relevant to the assigned tasks.

Team A group of people who organize themselves to work cooperatively on a common objective.

Team building Activities designed to improve a team's performance.

Transparent Information that anyone can access.

Trust To have confidence in or rely on the integrity and abilities of other people.

Virtual team *See* Distributed team.

Virtual world A simulated world that you can explore, manipulate, and affect.

Wiki A Web site that many users can contribute to by creating and editing the content.

Work breakdown structure (WBS) A diagram you use to organize project tasks.

Index

86–87

~~~uations~~~uations
  reviewing, 12–13
  self-, 12
example, setting an, 78–79
excellence, developing a reputation for, 74–75
expectations
  clarifying, 10–11, 62–63
  exceeding, 12–13
  understanding, 8–9